The Art of
Mail Armor

How to
Make
Your
Own

Mary Brewer
Foreword by Brian R. Price

PALADIN PRESS · BOULDER, COLORADO

The Art of Mail Armor
How to Make Your Own
by Mary Brewer

Copyright © 2002 by Mary Brewer

ISBN 1-58160-306-1
Printed in the United States of America

Published by Paladin Press, a division of
Paladin Enterprises, Inc.
Gunbarrel Tech Center
7077 Winchester Circle
Boulder, Colorado 80301 USA
+1.303.443.7250

Direct inquiries and/or orders to the above address.

PALADIN, PALADIN PRESS, and the "horse head" design
are trademarks belonging to Paladin Enterprises and
registered in United States Patent and Trademark Office.

Visit our Web site at: www.paladin-press.com

Table of Contents

Acknowledgments

I wish to thank the many people who have given me encouragement and help in completing this project. At the time I started this manuscript it seemed a simple little thing. It grew.

Pamela Hopkins and her students, especially Uhrs Chantell, provided so much help that it's hard to know where to begin to thank them. From scanning mail and diagrams to providing expertise and access to equipment, they did it all. I thank you very much!

Mike Riley of Switzerland provided not only the pictures of mail from museums, but many hours of encouragement as well. Mike, it was your request that started all this. Thank you from the bottom of my heart.

Kat Lan deserves a lot of thanks for her encouragement and expert advice. Your help was invaluable, Kat.

Tim O'Donnell gets special thanks also. Tim, you are a great editor and provided me with many ideas on areas that needed improvement. Thanks for your time and help.

Thanks to my models, David, Christine, Bill, Nikki and Jake Mead, and Raven. (Raven makes mail in New Mexico.)

Douglas Archer not only contributed some unique designs, but also supplied completed articles that are the very best quality. Thank you.

Kendra Milligan was helpful in scanning photos for this book.

Thanks to all my Internet Relay Chat (IRC) friends who put up with listening to technical discussions and general complaining and still gave me encouragement. Among them, Luk, Tim A. Parson, Jeff Garber, and Matthew J. Locke. You are great friends.

Gael Stirler, the CEO of Chivalry Sports in Tucson, Arizona, deserves the credit for finally getting this published. Than you for pointing me to a great company, Paladin. Of course Paladin itself deserves a great deal of thanks. Jon Ford, Donna DuVall, and many others did a great job producing a finished product.

Last but certainly not least, I want to thank Bill. Without you, Bill, I could not even have started. From support to technical knowledge, you have been my mainstay. Thank you.

I am sure that there is someone I've forgotten to mention. All I can say is, "Well, you know my memory! Thanks."

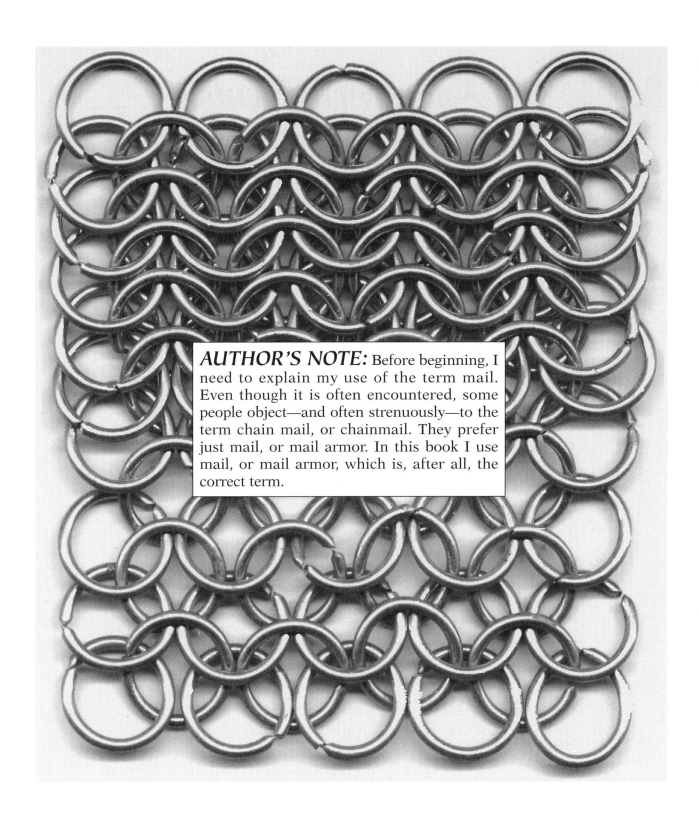

AUTHOR'S NOTE: Before beginning, I need to explain my use of the term mail. Even though it is often encountered, some people object—and often strenuously—to the term chain mail, or chainmail. They prefer just mail, or mail armor. In this book I use mail, or mail armor, which is, after all, the correct term.

Foreword

The study of arms and armour construction techniques has, since the Middle Ages, been the purview of a limited fraternity of metalworkers. Guarding their secrets with fervent ardor, armourers and metalworkers left us next to nothing besides limited examples of their work.

Anyone captured by the mystique of the knight in shining armour will likely find the tools and expertise needed to craft a harness of plate beyond his budget both in terms of time and money. Similarly, the complex armours of padded and stuffed cloth—also less than evocative of the knight's imagery—are surprisingly complex. But not all armour was of plate or cloth—for many centuries the knight of Europe was clad not in the brightly polished iron plate from *Excalibur* but in mail, the armour of linked rings adopted by the Roman cavalry that persisted as a cost-effective, functional, and very comfortable defense well into the 17th century.

The reasons for mail's persistence as an effective defense against bladed weapons lie in its relative ease of construction. Once the wire was extruded into suitable diameters it could be easily rolled into links using a variety of methods. European mail after the fall of Rome seems to have almost always been riveted or perhaps welded together, but the 4-in-1 pattern that predominated is easy enough that local production would have been possible throughout Europe both in highly efficient production centers and in smaller, localized operations.

For the modern student, mail represents a fine entrée into the world of armouring and, by extension, into the world of the medieval knight. Links can be simply woven and left butted; or, as the student progresses, more complex tailoring can be coupled with advanced methods of link closure such as spot-welding or, ultimately, riveting.

The secret to mail lies not in the techniques of link closure, but rather in the subtleties of pattern that the mailmaker must see in order to create smooth transitions of shape necessary to create garments and items of decorative jewelry.

It is precisely this that represents the strength of Mary Brewer's *The Art of Mail Armor*. Uncluttered by the current debates that surround various arcane questions concerning historical mail manufacture, her book presents a straightforward guide to the principles that underlie the creation of any mail garment.

Steeped in the tradition of the Renaissance Festival community so popular here in the United States, Ms. Brewer presents a host of techniques and patterns that demonstrate her roots. She has created nearly every form of mail accoutrement, garment, and curiosity, presenting both fundamentals and specifics she's used in her vast body of work.

For the novice, this work will represent a very easy to understand, clear presentation that will enable the casual student with just a few dollars to begin creating garments and objects of mail. The more experienced mailmaker will find tips on sizing, reduction, and tailoring more helpful, opening the doors to advanced study as the mailmaking community begins to experiment more seriously with the medieval methods of link closure and historical recreation.

Creating mail is much like knitting; for the person with the affinity and just a bit of diligence, there is a ready market amongst Renaissance Faire patrons, live-action role players, costume patrons, Medieval and Renaissance reenactors, tournament companions, collectors of arms and armour, and even in Hollywood.

Brian R. Price
Techniques of Medieval Armour Reproduction (Paladin Press)
The Knighthood, Chivalry & Tournaments Resource Library
http://www.chronique.com

Introduction

Now that you know what to call it, picture yourself in a full set of shining mail armor. And the best part of all is that you made the mail yourself! This manual will show you how to do just that.

Mail is made of wire formed into circles or rings and pieced together in an interlocking pattern. This manual shows you how to construct tools, change a straight piece of wire into rings, and assemble them to form mail. It contains complete instructions for making your own *coif* (head covering), *hauberk* (shirt), and *gauntlets* (gloves). There is also a section on designs for your edges and other decorative touches.

Mail is a very versatile medium. It can be used not only for armor but also for necklaces, bracelets, and belts. Different patterns, metals, and sizes of wire and links create endless flexibility and variety. A link is a circle of wire connected to other links to form a pattern. By making the links larger you can create a lacy effect that can make a beautiful bishop's collar, a necklace that goes from the neck to the tip of shoulder. Or you can make your links smaller and thicker to produce a heavy mesh material suitable for armor for actual combat. The thickness of wire is termed the *gauge*. Sixteen-gauge wire is relatively thin, whereas 14-gauge is medium, and 12-gauge is very thick.

Most people associate mail armor with the period between the 10th and 14th centuries, but it dates back long before that. Romans wore it long before A.D. 400. Although you can still see mail armor in museums, not a great deal of it remains because metal used in these earlier centuries did not stand up well to rust—not to mention arrows and dragons.

Antique mail was usually made with links forged shut or, in some cases, half of which were forged shut and half simply closed (butted).

Very ancient mail was made of links from square wire (looking similar to a thin washer). There were several versions of how they were closed. One is that the links were flattened and the ends overlapped. A hole was drilled through both sides of the ring and fastened with a rivet. As time went by makers of mail did not flatten the wire, which retained a square shape. Again, holes were drilled at each end of the link, but the links did not overlap. Instead, a fastener similar to a staple went through the links and connected the two ends, which were then forged in place.

The metal used in those days was not of the same quality as that we have today. It was much weaker and so pulled apart much more easily unless the ends were fastened. The consistency and strength of today's steel allows us to make very usable mail without welding the links shut or using rivets.

The purpose of this book is not to give you a history of mail, but rather a simple way to make your own mail. I will show you how to start with a piece of wire and end with a finished garment. In addition to showing you how to make attractive designs, I emphasize how to make mail as inexpensively as possible. But, as in the days of old, mail is still very expensive. A standard short-sleeved mail shirt costs at least $250—and usually more. Although it wears well and lasts a long time, that's still a pretty expensive garment. You can make your own for much less. What it will cost you is time.

If you wish to read about the history or armor, several excellent books are available on the subject. Among them are *A Glossary of the Construction, Decoration, and Use of Arms and Armour in All Countries and in All Times* by George Cameron Stone; *Phaeton Guide to Antique Weapons and Armour* by Robert Wilkinson-Latham; *Medieval Warfare Source Book Volume I: Warfare in Western Christendom* by David Nicolle; *Arms & Armor* by Michele Byam; *Warfare in the Classical World* by John Warry; and *An Historical Guide to Arms and Armor* by Stephen Bull.

Another source of information about armor is the Society for Creative Anachronism (SCA). Founded in 1966, SCA is dedicated to the study of the Medieval period. It now has more than 22,000 members, who conduct seminars, classes, and reenactments of the Middle Ages. The society also has several publications. You can contact SCA for a complete list and ordering information (P.O. Box 360789, Milpitas, CA 95036-0789 or online at www.sca.org).

To start, you need only a few supplies: some pieces of scrap wood to make a base for your winder, which is a machine you will construct to make your links; a steel rod to wind the links around; a good pair of wire cutters to cut the links; a scrap piece of heavy cloth or a glove to protect your hand; and two pairs of good needlenose pliers. Read Chapters 2 and 3 thoroughly before you attempt anything. These give you complete instructions for building your winder and several methods for cutting your links. The exact materials that you need depends on which method you choose. None of the items illustrated in this book require very expensive materials, except for the wire itself, and you will need considerable quantities of that. In Chapter 2, however, I give you some ideas on how to acquire less expensive wire.

Chapter 1 explains some terms and definitions and compares some ancient mail with some modern mail that I have made.

Chapters 2 and 3 tell you how to make links. Links are always closed with a twisting, sideways motion. Never open a link by making the diameter larger. If you do this you will lose the shape of the ring when you close it. If you cut your links on a slight diagonal, they will join together better. Just be careful with your closings and you will have a very useful mail item when you are done.

In Chapter 4 you begin to construct the most common pattern of mail, called 4-on-1. Each link has four links

My son, David, in his plate armor.

connecting through it. Most of the items illustrated in this manual are based on this pattern, although the techniques can be applied to other patterns. You will find that the "direction" in which the links are joined in is very important. Always check the diagrams to see whether you should go up or down through a link. The diagrams are large enough that you can see them easily. Notice that the pattern forms rows and columns. Rows consist of a link tilted away from you and a link tilted toward you, going across the mail. The columns consist of links all tilted in the same direction and going up and down. It is also important that you join the links in the proper order.

Chapter 5 shows you how to join two pieces of mail together, which is essential. Even for shirts, you can see that there are times when you need to go all the way around, as in an arm, and join at the seam. This will not only show you how to join a straight piece of mail but also mail at right angles and at a slant.

Chapters 6 through 9 cover techniques needed to make actual garments. These include showing you how to enlarge a piece, form points or V-shaped sections of mail, and round a square corner area. The last technique is used to form the edgings and to shape around the face and neck. I suggest you try constructing a small piece of mail in each of these areas to familiarize yourself with these techniques before starting a large project.

Chapters 8 and 9 tackle the problem of one side's being shorter than the other one. They show you how to increase or decrease the size of the mail as you make it. This could be used, for example, to form a trapezoid shape for arms and coifs.

In case you get tired of the 4-on-1 pattern, Chapters 10 and 11 teach you new patterns. In Chapter 10 you'll learn the 6-on-1 pattern, which is very similar to the 4-on-1 pattern but produces a much denser mail. Chapter 11 introduces you to a totally different new pattern, 6-on-2. This pattern forms a flowerlike design and uses two different ring sizes. It can be used as an edging or by itself to make stunning armor.

Chapter 12 gives you some ideas for the edges of your armor, as well as designs for inlaying four different crosses. Although this manual was written mainly for constructing armor, the basic techniques are the same for making crosses and other items of jewelry.

Chapter 13 contains complete instructions for making your own hauberk (shirt). It tells you how to take measurements, where to start, how to form the neck, and how to add the arms.

Designs for coifs (mail that covers the head) are given in Chapters 14 and 15. Chapter 14 teaches two ways to make a coif using a rounded method, while Chapter 15 shows how to make a coif using a square

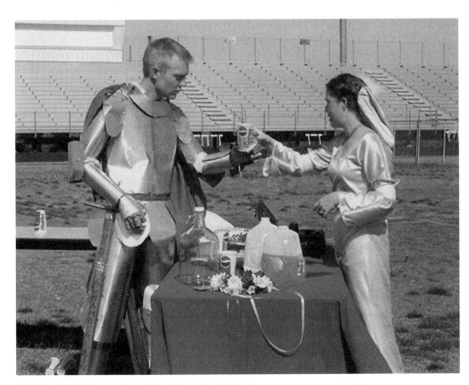

David and Trisha, my daughter, at a school festival.

*Trisha (left)
threading her way
through the crowd
at the Arizona
festival.*

construction method. The latter is my own design, and I think it is a great improvement on the rounded method, which usually leaves a hump at the point of the head. The chapter also has directions for making a bishop's mantle or bishop's collar.

Chapter 16 has a pattern for gauntlets (gloves). Gauntlets did not contain mail on the palm portion because mail would prevent the wearer from getting a good grip on a sword. Older gauntlets were shaped like mittens, and the first pattern is for that type. The same techniques are used to make gauntlets with individual fingers, and those instructions are included as well.

Chapter 17 provides some interesting ways to clean your mail. I, for one, hate to scrub, and I think these suggestions may eliminate some effort for you. Different metals require different methods. The chapter covers methods to easily clean steel, copper, and brass, a bonus for cleaning all those little trinkets around the house.

As a bonus, Chapter 18 gives detailed directions for different types of jewelry. Included are directions for headpieces, bracelets, necklaces, armbands, handflowers, half-gauntlets, and one of my own design called a shoulder necklace.

Chapter 19 discusses different types of mail. It also gives directions for making two types of 12-on-2 mail, bar mail, the wave pattern, and two types of Chinese chains. If you are looking for something different to add to a design, these provide interesting options to make it unique.

Chapter 20 is a photo gallery of different types of mail, both old and new. I hope you enjoy it.

• • •

I am not saying that the method presented here is the only way to make mail. I have found that if you learn this method completely, you will find it easier to form your own methods and techniques and to be able to understand descriptions of others methods more quickly.

Although I always found the Renaissance period fascinating, I didn't get involved with armor until my son and daughter started a Renaissance Society at their high school. As master of ceremonies for their annual festival, my son, David, needed something to wear. We started

Trisha at the Apache Junction Renaissance Festival.

looking at armor. What we ended up with was strictly for show. It consisted of a suit of plate armor made from aluminum press plates (they are used in printing newspapers). It definitely would not be any good in a battle, but it looked great.

For several years after that I was involved in the Renaissance Festival held at their school and attended the big Renaissance Festival in Apache Junction, Arizona.

About a year later I had an opportunity to take a two-hour class in mail construction given by a local store. Unfortunately, the classes were discontinued after one session. The technique I learned there seemed awkward to me, so I developed through trial and error what I consider a better method. I won't mention the hours it took to figure out how to shape and attach an arm or design the top of a coif. I read everything I could find on mail (which wasn't very much on actual construction techniques). Some of my friends on IRC asked me for instructions, which I wrote and e-mailed to different people. Someone mentioned that I should write a book. Thus, this manual was born.

I hope that you find the material useful and that it provides you with many hours of enjoyment—and maybe even a little profit.

CHAPTER 1

Some Terminology and Comparisons, Ancient and Modern

I t's always more fun to be able to refer to things by their proper names, so I've included a little list here along with some general information.

Many believe that mail was invented by the Celts in the 4th century B.C. and that the term *mail* is derived from the Latin term *macula*, which, among other things, means mesh of a net.

aketon, haketon (or gambeson): The padded garment worn under mail. It not only made mail more comfortable to wear but also added protection from blows. Although mail protects from a cut, because it is flexible it does not protect from bruising and broken bones.

aventail: The part of the coif that extends from one side and fits around the neck to protect it, fastening at the other side.

bishop's mantle (or bishop's collar): A wide necklace or collar of mail, sometimes separate, sometimes incorporated into the coif, to protect the neck and shoulders. It usually extended from around the neck to slightly over the shoulder and was designed to give extra protection to the neck, shoulder, and upper arms.

camail: The attachment at the bottom of a helmet that protects the neck area.

chausses: Mail made to protect the legs.

Figure 1-1. Close-up of mail from A.D. 1060 in Landes Museum, Zurich, Switzerland. (Courtesy of Mike Riley.)

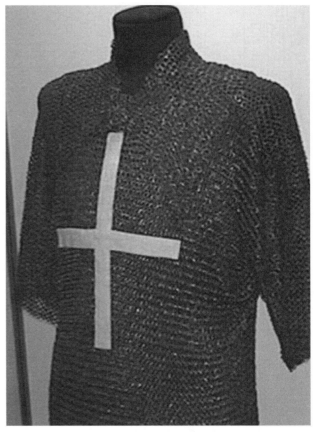

Figure 1-2. A 15th-century mail shirt from the Landes Museum. The cross is made of cloth and sewn onto the mail. (Courtesy of Mike Riley.)

coif: A piece of mail worn to protect the head, like a hood.

gauntlets: A pair of gloves. There were several types made. The earlier ones were similar to mittens. Usually these were attached to the sleeves on one side, toward the inside of the wrist, thus allowing the wearer to slide them off and let them dangle when not in use. Later more elaborate gauntlets were made with fingers, like a pair of modern gloves. Gauntlets were *never* made with mail on the inside of the fingers and palm area. You can't hold a spear or sword securely with metal on metal.

haubergeon: A shirt of mail, generally extending to the elbow and midthigh.

hauberk (or byrnie): A full-length defense of mail for the body, legs, and arm.

sabatons: A device to protect the top of the foot.

surcoat: A garment worn over mail, this was a loose, sleeveless piece of cloth believed to help keep the sun from heating the metal and making it too hot to wear. It was also believed to provide identification.

Finding records that show mail or how it was made in the early centuries is difficult. Most mail from this period has long

Figure 1-3. Close-up of mail from the Landes Museum from around A.D. 1400. (Courtesy of Mike Riley.)

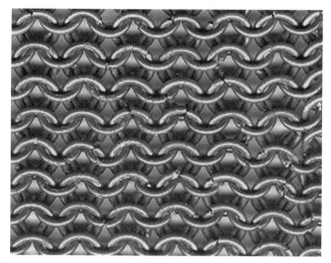

Figure 1-4. Modern mail made from coat hangers.

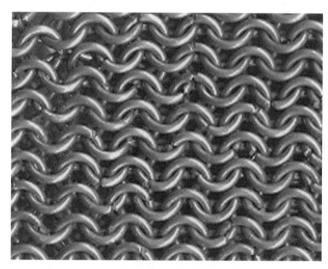

Figure 1-5. Modern mail made from welding rod.

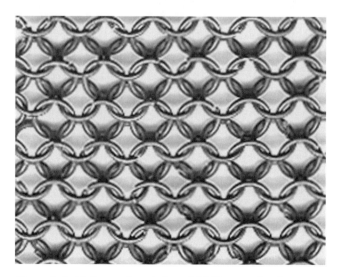

Figure 1-6. Modern mail made from 16 1/2-gauge tie wire.

since rusted away. Records of mail are more common from about the 11th century on.

Mail garments started out as vests or short-sleeved shirts. Gradually, they covered more and more until finally the sleeves were full length and had attached mittens with leather palms (gauntlets). Most early helmets sat on top of a coif; later some had mail attached around the bottom to protect the neck.

Gradually, the designers of mail started to fasten plates on top of the mail. First they attached breastplates. Next arm, shoulder, and leg guards were added until gradually a whole suit of plate mail was developed. Most suits were worn with mail underneath, at the shoulders and neck, and a skirt. The skirts were usually slit at the front and back to allow for horseback riding while still protecting the legs. (If it had been slit at the sides it would have bunched up near the top front of the saddle and at the back would not have been able to reach far enough around to even come close to the leg.) Only foot soldiers wore mail with slits at the sides, and not many could afford it.

Mail was not a poor man's possession. Even in those days it was expensive. A lord of the castle could usually afford it, and depending on how rich he was, he might possibly provide it for his knights as part of their pay, along with food and lodging.

I thought it would be interesting in this chapter to give you some comparisons between the mail you can make and the mail you can see in museums.

Figure 1-1 shows a closeup of mail from 1060. Notice that it was made with square wire and had rivets joining it together.

Figure 1-2 is of mail from around A.D. 1400. It was made with flat wire, not square, as in the older mail. Figure 1-3 shows mail from around 1500. Unfortunately, the close-ups of Figure 1-2 and 1-3 are not very clear, but they are the only ones I have.

Now, let's skip a few centuries and look at some current mail. Figure 1-4 is made from coat hangers, whereas Figure 1-5 shows mail made from welding rod and Figure 1-6 from 16 1/2-gauge tie wire.

The first thing you notice is the difference in density between the mail made from tie

Figure 1-7. A 14th-century hauberk from the Landesmuseum. (Courtesy of Mike Riley.)

Figure 1-8. A modern mail vest.

Figure 1-9. A 14th-century helmet with camail from the Landesmuseum. (Courtesy of Mike Riley.)

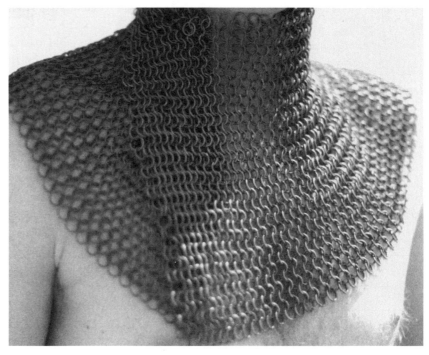

Figure 1-10. A close-up of a modern aventail of coif in 17-gauge tie wire.

wire and that made from coat hangers or welding rod. Both pieces were constructed with links made on the same size rod. The inside diameter of both types of links is the same, but the outside diameter is larger on the welding-rod mail because the wire is much thicker. Thus, when four links are threaded through one link it leaves much less extra space and produces much denser mail.

As for utility, the mail made today is probably much sturdier than the mail made earlier because of the better quality steel. I suppose if you really wanted to try to make mail that looked like that made in the 11th century, you might try using washers or lock washers. However, drilling holes in the links and putting in pins would be a huge job. Good luck.

Finally, yes, there are some differences between ancient mail and modern mail, but from a distance of several feet they are not that noticeable. And unless you can find and afford ancient mail, you don't really have much choice if you want mail.

CHAPTER 2

Wire Sizes and Types of Wire

This chapter contains a great deal of detailed information. You may find it a bit boring and be tempted to skip it until you actually need to use it. It does contain some specific information you will need in the beginning, so I recommend that you at least read it now and keep it handy to refer to when you need the information.

If your hands are tender, it might be easier for you to use a 16- or 16 1/2-gauge tie wire when you start out. This wire bends much more easily than 14-gauge steel, so it comes apart much more easily—for those annoying times when you find you joined a link onto the wrong link or in the wrong direction. It is also cheaper. A 2 1/2-pound roll of 16 1/2-gauge tie wire costs about $2.50 to $3.00 and can be purchased at any hardware store. The disadvantages to using 16- or 16 1/2-gauge wire are that the links must be closed very carefully or they will slide apart, and it is a little more difficult to see the pattern that you are forming. The links tend to fold back on one another and confuse you.

Although 16 1/2-gauge wire is not used very often for large mail pieces, it is easy and fast to work with and makes excellent mail for display or parade functions. When working with this gauge it is essential that you are extremely careful with the joinings because the wire is so thin that it can slip apart if any space is left, especially if two joinings hit against each other.

Naturally, you could weld the links together. This would require an acetylene-welding torch, with a pinpoint tip; regular solder is too soft and would crack and break with wear. You cannot weld together galvanized wire. With any other type of wire you can use the ends of the wire itself to melt together, or you can use a piece of the same wire to join it instead of a welding rod. It will give a bump at the join, very similar to that of ancient mail. Unless you have experience with welding, I do not recommend that you try this because it is a very large and expensive project. To give you an idea of the scope of such a project, an average shirt has approximately 25,000 rings in it.

Almost any type of wire can be used: bronze, copper, brass, galvanized steel, baling wire, stainless steel, or electric fence wire, to name a few. I have even heard of people using key rings. One place to find wire is at recyclers of junk metals. These places usually carry many different types of wire and are usually less expensive for copper and other of the more expensive metals.

Some types of metal (e.g., bronze) are prohibitively expensive. However, when used sparingly as an accent on edgings or for an inlaid design, they can be very impressive and worth the extra cost.

An excellent source of inexpensive wire is coat hangers. Most coat hangers are 14 1\2- or 14-gauge steel, but they do vary somewhat. When the varnish is cleaned off, they make beautiful polished-steel mail. A hint: Make the mail first and then clean the varnish off with paint remover by placing it in a glass jar, soaking it overnight, and then washing it off thoroughly. This takes less paint remover and is easier than manhandling clumsy coat hangers. CAUTION: *Paint remover can be very harmful to skin and eyes. Be careful and wear adequate protection.*

A cheaper method of cleaning the mail is to place it in a solution of four gallons of water and four cans of lye in a glass jar. This solution can be used for quite a few pieces of mail. Simply immerse the mail, let it sit for two or three days, and then remove it and wash it thoroughly. CAUTION: *Extreme care should be taken. Lye is very caustic and will burn your skin. Wear gloves and protective goggles.*

Lye will remove most paint but not plastic-based ones, as is sometimes used on coat hangers. Acetone or nail polish remover (which is basically acetone) will remove plastic-based paint. A little scouring powder, a stiff brush, and some elbow grease can remove any paint the lye missed. *Again, use caution with all chemicals.*

The most common gauge is 14 in steel, made in a link with an inside diameter of 3/8 inch. Another source of wire is 3/32-inch mild-steel welding rods. They come in 3-foot lengths, 14 rods to a pound, and can be purchased at any welding supply house. They cost approximately $1.50 a pound. *Do not use arc welding rods.*

One great thing about welding rods is that they come in different materials. Some bronze rods look just like brass . . . or gold! Using copper-coated welding rods is cheaper than using copper wire, and since they are harder, you can use 14-gauge in these rods. But 14-gauge copper wire bends easily, so mail made of it is not very strong.

With 14-gauge rods you get 42 feet to a pound. You can get approximately 26 to 27 rings per rod, depending on how careful you are with the ends. That's 364 to 378 rings per pound. This will make a piece of mail about 1 foot by 2 3/4 inches. So, 1 square foot of mail will take about 4 1/2 pounds of wire, or 189 feet, or 1,672 rings. A mail shirt takes approximately 15 square feet of mail, or about 25,000 links, depending on size and style. Remember, you have to allow for the gambeson (or aketon), the heavy padded garment worn underneath.

So, an average shirt requires about 68 pounds of wire. Figured at a cost of $1.50 a pound, a shirt costs approximately $102 in materials if you use welding rods.

Electric fence wire can be purchased in 1/4- or 1/2-mile rolls. This galvanized-steel wire is made of a softer steel than that used for coat hangers or welding rods but strong enough for mail. It is a little easier to work with and therefore a good material for beginners. It comes in 14- and 17-gauge. I highly recommend the 14-gauge. A 1/4-mile roll costs about $20; a 1/2-mile roll approximately $40. A 1/2-mile roll will make a shirt and is much cheaper than welding rods. The brass-colored welding rods make great accents to trim the silver-colored shirt.

The one question I get asked most often is, "How long does it take to make a shirt?" The answer is that it depends on many factors, such as how fast you work. I usually take my time, and you may be a lot faster than I am. The following is based on using 14-gauge electric fence wire and method three (see Chapter 2) for cutting links.

I can wind approximately 2,400 links in an hour and cut approximately 1,300 in the same amount of time. I can close about 800 in an hour. In one hour I can assemble a piece of mail about 1 foot by 4 inches.

If a square foot of mail contains approximately 1,700 rings, I spend approximately 3/4 hour winding, 1 1/4 hours cutting, and 2 hours opening links, for a total of 4 hours so far. Add about 3 hours to knit the square foot of mail. Thus, a square foot of mail requires about 7 hours of work. For a shirt requiring 15 square feet of mail you can figure on about 105 hours. Of course, you lose time making adjustments around the sleeves, etc. Don't get discouraged. You can always start out with a short-sleeved, waist-length vest and add to it later.

If you want to get into something heavier, you can use 12-gauge steel, 33 feet to a pound, with rings having an inside diameter of 1/2 inch. In welding rods this is called 1/7-inch mild steel. When you go to a heavier gauge of wire it is thicker, so you must increase the diameter of the ring to allow the other rings to pass through their middle.

To start we will work with 4-on-1 mail. This means that every link has four links going through it. Or to put it another way, every link goes through four other links, except on the edges. You will find most mail made in this pattern. Still with me? OK, let's get started.

WINDER

The first thing to do is to make your links. If you are experimenting, wind the wire around a pen, but for any serious project a piece of equipment known as a winder makes life much easier and faster (Figure 2-1).

As you can see from the drawing, the winder is relatively simple: a steel rod of 3/8-inch diameter (approximately $2 to $3 at a hardware store), placed through two boards on a base. The boards holding the rod should not be more than an inch tall or a wobble will develop when you wind. The handle on the end of the rod can be anything you want. Vise grips work well, or you can drill a hole through the rod and use a screw to attach a metal or wooden handle. Another option is to bend the rod itself in

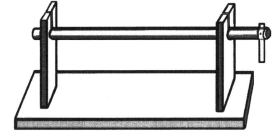

Figure 2-1.

two right angles (somewhat like a flattened Z) to form the handle from the rod. Bending the rod can be a little difficult.

Make a vertical cut from the top of each board down to the rod. The winder can then be clamped onto a table or bench for stability, with the handle over the edge to allow for turning. The length of the rod between the upright boards should be 6 inches. Next you must drill a hole through the rod to hold the end of the wire when you start to wind it. This hole is in the end of the middle section of the winder, near the end with the handle. Mark on the rod the point 1\4 inch from the vertical board next to the handle and between the two boards. This winder is used only for cutting method two. I suggest you read ahead about this method before constructing your winding machine.

Figure 2-2 shows another method of constructing a winder. Using screw-in steel eyelets or steel brackets instead of boards to hold the rod in place makes a much more stable winder. Take a stroll through your local hardware store; I am sure you will find a suitable bracket or screw-in eyelets (like the thing a screen door hook latches into). These eyelets come in all sizes (be sure the inside diameter is large enough for your rod to fit through) and are very easy to install. There is the definite advantage that the right-angle steel brackets or eyelets are fastened down with screws, which hold more securely than nails do under the pressure exerted. For stability, be sure that each

bracket has at least two points to attach to the
portion that meets the bottom board.

Again, you must drill a hole through the
rod to hold your wire in place when you start
to wind it, as shown in Figure 2-2. Also
notice the short length of pipe that is placed
between the handle and the first bracket. As
you wind you tend to push toward the

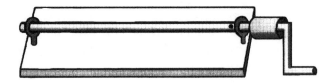

Figure 2-2.

winder. This piece of pipe around the rod prevents the handle portion from moving in and
hitting on the base, yet allows free movement of the rod.

You put the end of the wire through the hole in the rod. Don't go all the way through, just
past the far side of the hole. Turn the rod and your wire will coil around. The coils should be
right next to each other, like a spring. It helps to wear a glove on your left hand or use a bit of
cloth or leather to hold and guide the wire onto the rod. You need to put some tension on it, but
not very much. Each turn around the rod makes one link.

If you mount your rod so that the bottom of the rod is 1/2 inch above the board, when
winding you can use a large cable clamp (see Chapter 3) to help you finish winding that last
little bit of wire in each coil. To do this, simply place the cable clamp beneath the rod and let
the tag end of the wire feed through two of the prongs. Press down on the rod and turn the
handle. The wire will feed through and coil tightly on the rod. This only works for the ends of
the coils. If you try to do the whole coil this way, you must constantly move the cable clamp to
keep the coils from overlapping or spreading out too far (Figure 2-3).

If you decide that you want to make a large project, you will need many rings. Winding
them by hand can be tiresome and time consuming. An easy solution is to use an electric drill
to turn your rod. It is very quick and easy, but there are a few precautions you should take.

If you have tried winding by hand you know that it is very easy to have one
loop in the coil jump over on top of the previous one. In
this case, you can simply back it up and continue
the coil again. When you use an electric drill, you
are coiling very fast. If one loop jumps over on
top of another loop, it really makes a mess.

Other problems in using a drill for winding
are that the loops can get spaced too far apart and
unevenly and that your hands can be burned by
the wire going through them. The solution is to use a
guide for the wire and a holder for the spool of wire,
thus eliminating having to hold the wire altogether.

When you use an electric drill to wind your wire coil, use a
variable-speed reversible drill. (You may want to coil it in the
reverse mode. Some people prefer to feed the wire to the underside
of the rod.) Either way, the guide will ensure that each loop stays in line and does not jump on
top of the previous one.

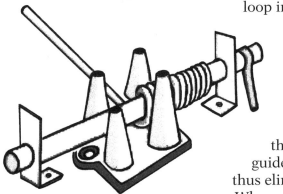

Figure 2-3.

The rod you use for winding with a drill is different from that previously described. The hole to
hold the wire to start winding is only about 2 inches from the end of the rod. You only need enough
of the rod sticking out to put in the chuck of the drill and for the first bracket of the winder.

Making a lot of links means you will be working from a spool of wire. You need to construct
a holder for the spool you coil from to allow a fast, smooth feed of wire to the rod. This also
provides just the right amount of tension on the wire to make it coil correctly without holding
the wire as it coils.

Place a metal rod through the spool and support the ends of the rod in notches on wooden
blocks. I suggest blocks because you don't want the rod to move sideways, thus dumping your

spool on the floor. Short pieces of 2 x 4 lumber works fine. The blocks can be connected by a bottom board and a side brace. Be sure the block construction is wide enough so that it will not interfere with the movement of the spool.

This holder is placed on the floor directly below the winder, which is clamped to your table. Place it so that the wire feeds up to the front of the rod, not the middle. You want a small amount of tension toward the front of the winder so that your guide will not pull toward the back and space the loops far apart.

A simple guide can be constructed from a rectangular piece of light metal about 6 inches by 3 inches. You can purchase a piece of galvanized metal called a tie plate at the local lumber or hardware store. It should cost under a dollar.

You want the guide to be about 3 inches wide along your winding bar so that the guide is stable and slides smoothly. If you make it too short it will "catch" instead of slide. When constructing this, you will get a better idea of what you are doing if you look at all the illustrations of the guide in this book *before* you begin.

Start by placing the middle of the metal strip on the winding bar and bending it around it. Use a pair of needlenose vise grips to crimp the strip down as tightly as possible and then use a hammer to beat it down around the rod (see Figure 2-4).

Now bend the two "legs." This is necessary to keep the guide from turning on the rod and also makes it slide along the rod more smoothly. The legs will slide along the bottom board of your winder, one of them along the closest edge to provide the correct slant for the wire to feed up. You don't want your wire to feed at a right angle because this will cause too much tension for your winder and drill to handle.

The legs must be "turned up" to prevent them from digging into the bottom board of your winder as they move. It is also advisable to turn up the ends away from the drill for the same reason. The smoother these slide, the less trouble you will have (Figure 2-5).

Separate the two legs to form an angle. To get a smooth fit put the guide on the rod. Next, bend the legs to form the turned-up area (Figure 2-6). Now bend one leg up to form a curl from your middle loop on the side away from you.

Bend the other side of the guide up to provide a smooth edge. I find that beating it down with a hammer is the easiest way. You want this edge fairly flat. I also use a hammer to bend the back edge of the guide up slightly. This way it cannot catch on the board as it slides.

Take it off the rod and drill two sets of holes through it right below the rod area. These will have bolts going through them to keep the guide from jumping off the rod. Remember, there is a lot of pressure exerted by the wire as it is winding. The holes should be at the front and back

Figure 2-4.   *Figure 2-5.*

of the guide. The front hole should be as close to the front as you can make it because it must contain a loop to feed the wire through (Figure 2-7).

The loop to feed your wire must extend just beyond the end of your guide. You can make this loop by twisting heavy wire first around your bolt, then around a loop sticking out from there, and finally back around the bolt. Another way is to drill two holes in a small piece of metal, one for the bolt and one to feed the wire through.

Figure 2-8 shows the beginning of a coil being wound.

Start out slowly until you get the hang of it. Remember to have a firm hold on your drill. There is quite a bit of force used in winding, and the drill will kick and try to turn when you start up. So brace the handle toward you on the table and hold it steady.

After winding the links (Figure 2-9), you must cut them. There are several ways to do this, and you will have to experiment to see which is best for you. The design of your winder will determine which method you choose. All of this is explained in the next chapter.

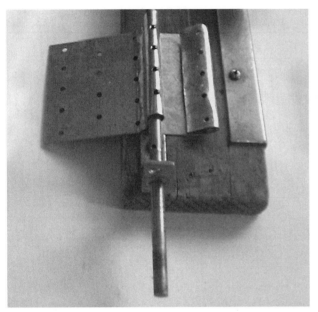

Figure 2-6.

Figure 2-7.

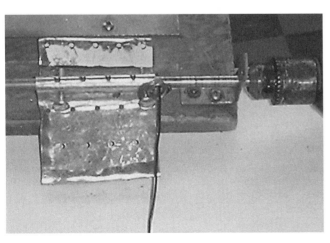

Figure 2-8.

Figure 2-9.

CHAPTER 3

Cutting Links

This chapter describes three methods of cutting your links. Because every person is different, what is easiest for one person is not necessarily easiest for another. I suggest that you read through all three methods before you decide to try one. But, remember, the most important rule for all three methods is to be safe! Wear goggles and gloves when necessary.

I have found that, overall, method three is easiest for me. I travel quite a bit and do not always have easy access to electricity. I have also reached the age where my joints complain bitterly when under stress, especially when I use a hacksaw. So I exert myself as little as possible. (I am naturally lazy.)

METHOD 1

Pull the end of the wire from the hole in the rod. Slip the coil off the rod. Take some heavy wire cutters and clip each ring from the coil.

This method is very hard on your hands. If you insist on using it, I recommend that you find a good-quality cutter, with long handles, and grind down the jaws of the cutters to make them shorter. You get better leverage that way.

METHOD 2

Mike Riley of Switzerland developed this method, which works very well for him using a hacksaw. See the slots at the tops of the upright boards going down to the rod (Figure 3-1). Yes, these form a guide for the hacksaw. Leave the wire coil attached on the rod, just the way you finished winding it. Slip the hacksaw in the grooves and hack away. Of course, when you set up your winder, be sure that the length of the rod allows for movement of the hacksaw.

For a variation of the above, use a drill with a thin grinding disk or a Dremel tool on it. The disk must be thin, or else the gap in your links will be too large to close properly.

If you use this method, I suggest mounting another parallel rod to guide your cut. When you use cutting disks, remember that if they are not kept at

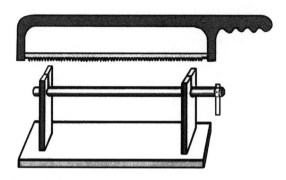

Figure 3-1.

right angles to the coil the blade will catch and shatter the disk or lash back, which can end up cutting something you don't want cut—such as you! *This is very dangerous; wear protective goggles.*

I occasionally use method two with a diamond-cutting wheel. I found it was easier to make the cuts if I removed the coil from the winder and positioned it on a rod and then placed this on a piece of wood that I had hollowed out to fit the coil and hold it in place. This was then placed in a small plastic tray full of water, with blocks at the ends to hold the coil together tightly. These blocks are important, even though I didn't include them in the drawings Figure 3-2. You can also use vise grips to hold the ends in place. If you do not have the ends blocked, when you cut through a link it tends to flip out and catch on the wheel.

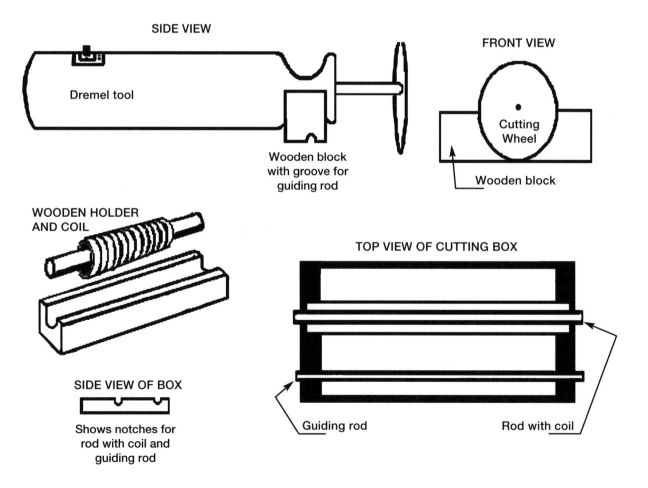

Figure 3-2.

The water in the tray cools the wire and wheel while cutting and acts as a bit of a lubricant as well.

I also mounted a guide bar for the Dremel tool and put a square attachment on the tool to keep it at right angles. The water is a little messy (you can put a shield up to prevent spattering), but it keeps your cutting wheel cool and provides some lubrication. *Be sure to wear protective glasses!*

After considerable experimentation with this method, I felt that it wasn't worth my effort. Also, the blades for the Dremel tool get expensive (it uses diamond cutting blades) and wear out quickly. I went back to method three, which I find faster, cheaper, and easier.

METHOD 3

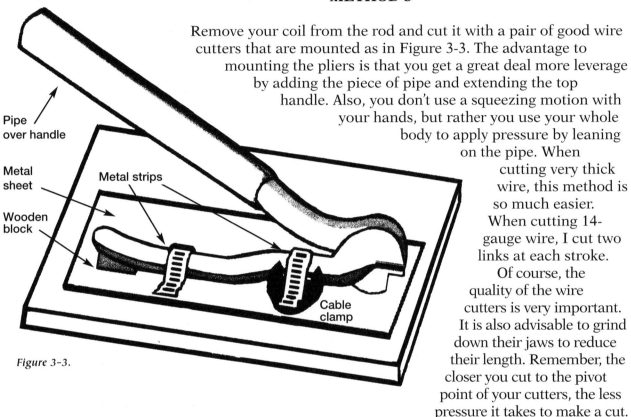

Remove your coil from the rod and cut it with a pair of good wire cutters that are mounted as in Figure 3-3. The advantage to mounting the pliers is that you get a great deal more leverage by adding the piece of pipe and extending the top handle. Also, you don't use a squeezing motion with your hands, but rather you use your whole body to apply pressure by leaning on the pipe. When cutting very thick wire, this method is so much easier. When cutting 14-gauge wire, I cut two links at each stroke. Of course, the quality of the wire cutters is very important. It is also advisable to grind down their jaws to reduce their length. Remember, the closer you cut to the pivot point of your cutters, the less pressure it takes to make a cut.

Pipe over handle

Metal sheet

Metal strips

Wooden block

Cable clamp

Figure 3-3.

They must be mounted in a very stable way (Figure 3-3). I took a baseboard (you can use the same one you mounted your winder on) and placed a thin metal sheet on the area underneath the cutters. Wood tends to "give," and this prevents the cutters' handles from wearing into the board and everything coming loose. If this happens, the cutters will not cut properly. So, if you are having problems cutting, check to see whether there is movement of the cutters when you apply pressure.

For mounting the nose end of the cutters, I used a cable wire clamp (Figure 3-4), which you can find at any hardware store. I ground the four prongs down until they were below the level of the bottom handle of the cutters when they are on their side. The U-shaped bolt piece is not used.

Take a close look at the way the jaws of your cutters move when you open them. The bottom jaw drops down at the pivot point. Open and close the jaws several times as you watch. You must allow for this movement, which is why you are using a clamp to raise the cutters slightly above the

Figure 3-4.

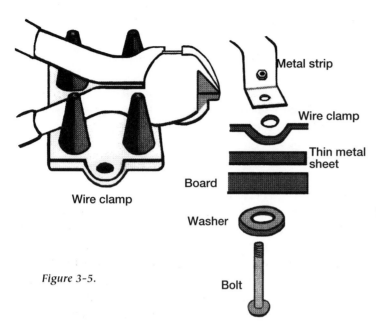

Figure 3-5.

Metal strip

Wire clamp

Thin metal sheet

Board

Washer

Bolt

Wire clamp

board, as well as holding them in place. The clamp must be positioned *behind* where the jaw moves (Figure 3-5).

Also, drill holes in your baseboard to fasten the cutters at the lowest curve of the bottom handle. If your cutter handles come back up at the handle end (most do, but some don't), you need a brace there. The easiest way is to put a wooden wedge at the end of the handle. Another way is to drill a hole directly under this point and put a nut and washer on it, adding washers till you reach the right height (refer to Figure 3-3).

OK. You have ground down the prongs on the clamp and the jaws of your cutters. Next, you drill matching holes in your board for the clamp. I also make a recess in the bottom of the board so that the washer and the head of the bolt don't stick out. This way the bottom is flat and easy to clamp on a table or bench. If you don't want to do this, you can simply add strips of wood to the bottom of the baseboard, making a frame that holds the board above the bolts.

I have mentioned grinding down the nose of your cutters. Figure 3-6 shows such a ground-down nose. Notice that the bottom jaw is ground in parallel to the cutting edge for a short distance. This allows you to slide the coil of wire in farther and to position the wire more easily.

You can usually cut two to three links at a time with this adjustment. Without this cut, if you try to cut more than one link at a time, it tends to spread and misshape your rings.

You will need two strips of thin metal to loop over the handles to fasten them down. It must be thin because you have very little allowance between the handles at the jaw end of the cutters, and you have to go between them.

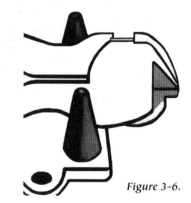

Figure 3-6.

Front Assembly

From the bottom, place a large washer on the bolt and feed the bolt through the hole in the board. Place a metal plate on the bolt. Place wire clamp on the bolt. Place a thin strip of metal on the bolt; put on the nut and tighten. Do the other side the same way, making sure your metal strip is tight.

Now bolt down your cutters at the points farther back on the bottom handle and make sure there is no movement. Do *not* use nails: they will loosen and come out.

LINKS, OPENED AND CLOSED

Now that you have some links made, you need to divide them into two types: closed links and open links. Remember that links are opened and closed by twisting them in a sideways motion, never by making the diameter larger.

To close a link of heavy metal, use two pairs of pliers, preferably needlenose. I use a straight needlenose pair in my left hand and a pair of curved needlenose in my right (Figure 3-7).

Hold one pair with the handles facing up in your left hand. This seems a little awkward at first, but with a little practice it is very handy. Holding the pliers in this manner and using a

Figure 3-7.

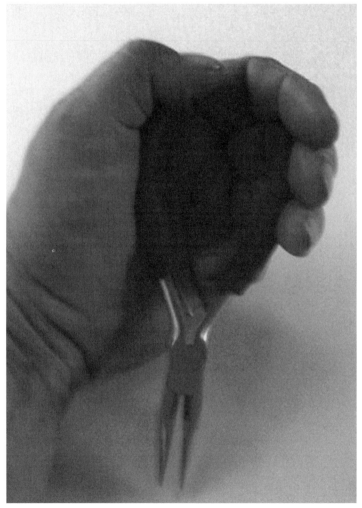

Figure 3-8.

curved pair of pliers in your right hand give you a much better field of vision when working (Figure 3-8).

It is also handy to use pliers that have a spring built in that causes the pliers to open automatically. This way you do not have to keep one finger bent in between the handles to push them open.

Place a link, opening up, in the pliers in your left hand, gripping across the link. Take the other pair of pliers normally in your right hand and grip parallel to others, covering about one-third of the link. Twist the link closed.

To avoid leaving scratches from the pliers on your mail, you can put a piece of masking or adhesive tape or a piece of felt or even some silicone on the inside of the pliers jaws. I don't find this necessary when using hard steel.

About half your links should be closed. If you are thinking of welding them shut, it might be a good idea to do this now. That way, you will get half of the links done without having to wrestle with a large, awkward piece of mail. Naturally, you will still have to do the other links after the mail has been assembled. But be prepared to put in a great deal more work and time with this method. Good luck.

Open links need to be open enough to fit over the other links. Unfortunately, when you cut your links from a coil, they end up not quite open enough. There are several ways of solving this. You can just open them a little, or you can stretch your coil a little, like a spring, before cutting the links. This isn't practical with very heavy wire, but it works great with the 16 1/2-gauge wire. Another idea is to coil two wires at once when you are winding. This takes a little practice, but it spaces the openings perfectly.

4-on-1
Mail Pattern

In describing how to assemble mail, I use two terms you need to keep straight: *row* and *column*. Rows go across; columns go up and down (Figure 4-1). This gives us a reference point . . . just as on a graph. I can say "row 5, column 6," and you will know the exact link to which I am referring.

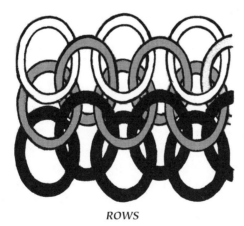

ROWS

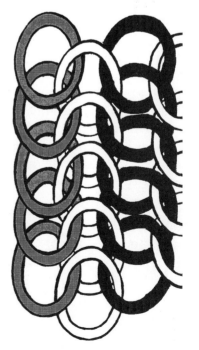

COLUMNS

Figure 4-1.

ROWS: *The black and gray links are each one row. The white links are the edge and do not count as a row. Always count rows from the open ring and the last closed ring added to it.*

COLUMNS: *The black and gray links are closed rings. The white links are open rings*

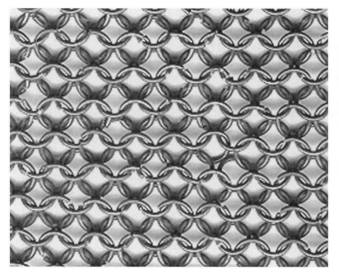

Figure 4-2.

Figure 4-3.

Remember that mail is a pattern. If you get the basics of the pattern fixed in your mind, you will have much less trouble learning it. Every other column of links slants in the same direction. So, odd-numbered columns (i.e., 1, 3, 5, 7) all slant up toward you and are closed rings. Even-numbered columns (i.e., 2, 4, 6, 8) slant down toward you and are open rings. So, rows going across alternate, one up, one down, and so on, as illustrated in Figure 4-1.

You will read this often in this book: the direction the links lie in is important. It's like knowing the direction in which you are traveling—it makes it much easier to get there!

We start off with the 4-on-1 pattern of mail. This means that each link has four links going through it, or to put it another way, each link goes through four other links. Figures 4-2 and 4-3 show some actual mail. Look closely and study the row and columns.

In Figure 4-4, your first step is to take one open link, shown in black in the figure, and place *four* closed links on it. Close this open link. Notice that you now have one closed link (black) with four links on it.

Figure 4-4

In Figure 4-5, you take one open link (black), place two closed links on it, and then thread this open link through two of the four closed links you had in the first set you did in Figure 4-4. Again, notice that you have another black ring, which you will close, going through four other rings.

Figure 4-5

Continue this step until you have a chain of links in this pattern: 2, 1, 2, 1, 2, 1 , 2 . . . until you reach the desired length of the mail. Lay the chain out so that the links alternate in direction, with the columns of two links tilted so that the bottoms are up toward you and the columns of single links having their bottoms down nearest you. (Check Figure 4-1 to see how columns and rows run.)

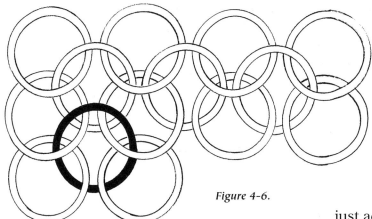

Figure 4-6 illustrates the step that is used at the beginning of every row. Take one open link, place two closed links on it, and join through the bottom of the first set of two links, column one, and the bottom of the set of two links in column three. Yes, you connect to every other column. Be careful that your links are laid in the proper direction and intersect from the proper side.

Figure 4-6.

Again, the open ring that you have just added is going through four rings. One way to count them as you are doing it is to say, "On my open ring I place two closed rings, and then I go up through the bottom left ring for the third ring, and then up through the bottom right ring for the fourth ring." Counting the rings you put on each open ring might help in the beginning.

Notice that all the links in odd-numbered columns are the closed links that you just added. Also, all the links in the even-numbered columns are the open links you added and closed.

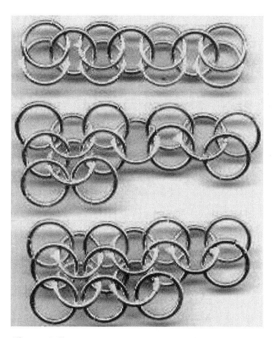

Figure 4-7.

It might be easiest when you are starting to use this method to hold the open link with the two closed links on it in your right hand. Take the left side of the open link and thread it up through the bottom link in column 1. Then grasp the open link with your left hand and thread the right-hand side of the link up through the bottom link in column 3. Close the link. At this point I must stress the importance of keeping your links "facing" in the proper direction. Later, when you are familiar with how to do this, you will not need to be so deliberate. It will become second nature.

Figure 4-7 illustrates the first three steps of construction in a piece of actual mail in 14-gauge steel.

OK, to reiterate, you can fiddle with the closed link in column 1 or 3 that you just put on. Try moving an end link. If it is folded back under the link in column 2, for example, you lose all track of how things go. So make sure the end link is out all the way to the right for column 3 and to the left for column 1, and presto! The pattern is intact.

Again, if you are having trouble seeing this, go back to Figure 4-1 and study the pattern of columns and rows. You must have this firmly fixed in your mind, or else you will become confused when working more complex mail.

Notice that your 4-on-1 pattern has already become obvious. If you get confused—and sooner or later you will—stop and look at the mail surrounding the area you are working. If you keep in mind the overall pattern, it should give you an idea of where you are going wrong. Remember to look for your columns and rows.

For Figure 4-8, take one open link, put one closed link on it, thread the left-hand side up through the last two links of column 3 (yep, that one you were just playing with is the first one), and thread the right-hand side of the open link up through the bottom link of column 5.

Again, notice that you are going through four links with the open link you are adding: one closed link on the open link, up through the two links on the left to make three links, and then up through the link on the right to make four links on the open link you are adding.

Now, just continue the step in Figure 4-8 until you reach the end of the row. Then start your next row with step three, shown in Figure 4-6, and continue with step four, shown in Figure 4-8, until you reach the end of that row. And on, and on, until you end up with whatever you want. It's a lot like crocheting with iron.

Of course, there are a few more things you need to know. Before getting into them, I suggest that you make a large piece of mail, at least 1 foot square, so that you become completely familiar with the process. It is essential that you learn this part completely before you try to learn reductions or increases. You will only get confused if you don't have the basic pattern down. When you feel that you can do it in your sleep (not recommended because it tends to tear up your sheets), then you move on.

Figure 4-8.

So you made your square of mail. Now you ask, "What am I going to do with it?" Scrunched up, it makes a neat doorstop. It's kind of fun to just play with. However, it doesn't make a very good hot pad or seat cushion! Be that as it may, let's get on to something more practical.

If you have been working with just the 16- or 16 1/2-gauge wire, I recommend that you try some 14-gauge. There is a world of difference. The mail is much heavier and is a little more difficult to bend the links together. You definitely need two pairs of pliers to join the links.

One last thing I want to mention: mail is reversible. Turn it over and it looks the same on the other side. Turn it upside down—it's the same. The only difference you will find is in the direction of your columns if you turn it over from left to right.

Next try working on it with the odd-numbered columns facing down toward you. The only difference is that you add the closed ring after you go through the rings in the main piece of mail, instead of having the closed ring on your open ring to begin with. A little experimenting will show you why. You might even decide you like working from this angle better. It provides a "tunnel" down through the links for your pliers that can be very handy when working in thick wire.

CHAPTER 5

Joining

ACROSS

Joining two pieces of mail is essential at times—in which case you need two pieces of mail. So get to work!

Figure 5-1 shows two pieces side by side. Be sure to line them up correctly. Again, watch the directions of your columns. They have to continue from one piece to the other in the same direction. You are going to add the missing row between them and, in so doing, join them together.

For the mail in Figure 5-2, take one open link, go up through the bottom link of columns one and

Figure 5-1.

three of the top piece of mail, and then again up through the top links of columns one and three in the bottom piece of mail. Close the link, thus "stitching" the mail together. So your next link joins the bottom link of columns 3 and 5 in the upper piece and the top links of columns 3 and 5 in the lower piece of mail. The next ring joins columns 5 and 7 in the same way, and so on to the end on the row.

DOWN

Use the same method to join the ends of rows together. You are going to add the missing row, thus connecting the two pieces together.

Figure 5-3 shows two pieces of mail with their row ends lined up. Make sure your columns are facing the same direction.

Figure 5-2.

Figure 5-4 shows the first joining ring going up through the last two links (first piece of mail) and the first two links (second piece of mail) of row one of both pieces. The next joining link goes through the links in the end and beginning in rows 2 and 3.

Figure 5-5 shows how the next connecting link goes through end links in rows 3 and 4 on both pieces of mail. Continue this until both pieces are joined.

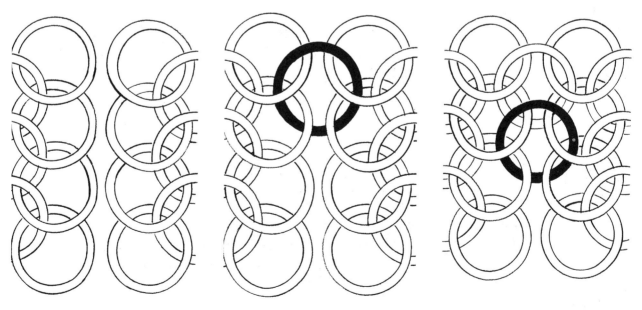

Figure 5-3.   *Figure 5-4.*   *Figure 5-5.*

Figure 5-6.

Figure 5-7.

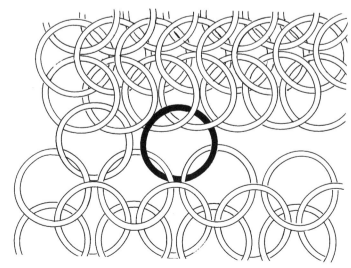

Figure 5-8.

AT RIGHT ANGLES

There are times when you want to join mail at a right angle. By this I mean that in one piece the rows go up and down and in the other piece the rows go across. This is used in the construction of coifs in the square method and also under the arms in the shirt.

First you start off with two pieces of mail, as in Figure 5-6. As usual, be sure that your pieces are laid out as in the diagram.

The first ring to join the two pieces will go up through the rings in columns 1 and 3 and through the last two rings in the top piece (see Figure 5-7).

The next ring will go up through the rings in columns 3 and 5 and through the next two rings in the top piece (see Figure 5-8).

This is continued all the way across the area you wish to join. Notice that when you go through the rings in the top piece of mail you do *not* go through the ring you connected with the last ring.

AT A SLANT

At times, such as on the sleeves, you will want to join a slanted piece of mail to a regular piece of mail. By a slanted piece I mean one that is gradually reduced, as the sides of a point are reduced (Figure 5-9). For easy reference about how to join any type of mail together, I am including it in this chapter. Reduction is covered in Chapter 7—you might want to skip this section until after you have read Chapter 7. Or even better, come back and reread this section after you finish Chapter 7.

Figure 5-10 shows the two types of mail side by side. As you can see, the one on the left is slanted, where the rows are gradually shortened.

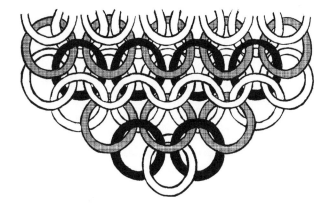

Figure 5-9.

Figure 5-10.

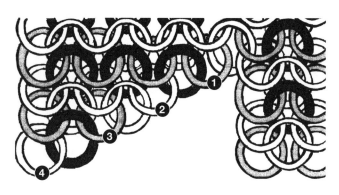

Figure 5-11.

Figure 5-12.

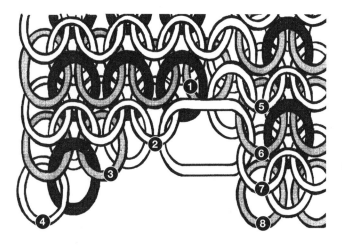

Figure 5-13.

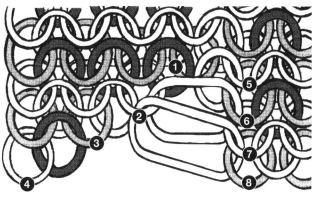

Figure 5-14.

Figure 5-11 shows the first ring joining the two pieces. It is placed up through the two links at the end of the first row in the left-hand piece of mail and up through the two links at the end of the right-hand piece of mail. This is the same as joining two regular pieces of mail together.

Figure 5-12 illustrates the next step. Let's start with the piece on the right. Go up through the third ring and the bottom ring, second ring, that you caught with the last joining ring labeled 6 and 5 on the diagram. On the piece of mail on the left, you go up through the bottom ring that you went through with the last joining ring, marked as 1 on the diagram. You are catching only three rings together, instead of the normal four.

Mail has a flexibility that drawings don't. As you join these pieces of mail, they will slide together. But for clarity I elongate the rings in the drawings so that you can see where they connect in relationship to the original links. Remember that although the drawings look a little funny, all links are the same size.

The links labeled 1, 2, 3, and 4 are the links of the left-hand piece of mail that will be used to join to the right-hand piece of mail. Each of these links will eventually have two links going through them, connecting them all together to three links from the right-hand piece of mail labeled 5, 6, 7, and 8. Notice that all these links are the ones that are angled up toward you, just as the links in the right-hand piece of mail are angled up toward you.

To continue, the next link is shown in Figure 5-13. This takes the next link in the right-hand piece of mail and the link above it (which you used in the last link) labeled 7 and 6 going up through them, and joins them to the link labeled 2 in the left-hand piece of mail.

The next link is added as in Figure 5-14. Go up through the next link and the last link you went through in the right-hand piece of mail and again through the link labeled 2, the same as in the last joining.

These same steps would be used to join the next links in the right-hand piece of mail labeled 8 and 7 to the rings in the left piece labeled 3 and 4. The thing to remember is to fasten to the rings that are slanted up toward you. If you try to fasten to the other rings, you will get a ring that stands up sideways and doesn't allow for movement.

CHAPTER 6

Extending

What happens if you find that the piece you made is too short or that you have gained weight? Just add to it. This section shows you how to extend your mail and make it wider.

Figure 6-1 shows you how to add one open link with two closed links on it to the first row of the mail that you have already made. Simply take your open link with two closed links on it and go up through the second and then the first ring in your original mail. Close the open link.

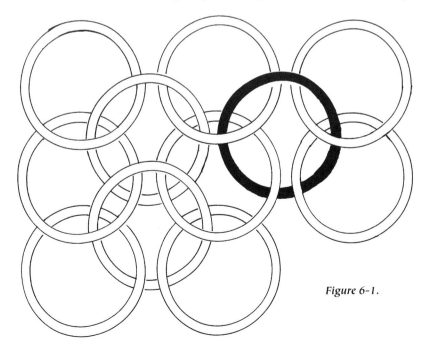

Figure 6-1.

Figure 6-2 shows how you can add more links to these rows, just as you made your original chain, until you reach the length you want to extend. You can add as many columns as you wish to make the desired length to the row.

Figure 6-3 shows the adding of the first rings in row two of the extended part of mail. Take an open link with one closed link on it and go up through the third link of the last column of your original mail and up through the second link of that column. Then go up through the second column of the new addition. Close your link.

Figure 6-4 shows the row finished. The following rows are done in the same way. Continue in this manner until you have the desired size.

Figure 6-2.

Figure 6-3.

Figure 6-4.

CHAPTER 7

Points and Rounding

POINTS—DOWN

Sometimes you want a piece of mail to gradually narrow to a point. This is not only useful for making edgings, but also for use around such areas as the face.

As usual, we start with a piece of mail, as shown in Figure 7-1. To start narrowing the mail, on the next row we begin with only one closed

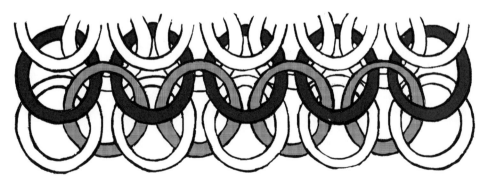

Figure 7-1.

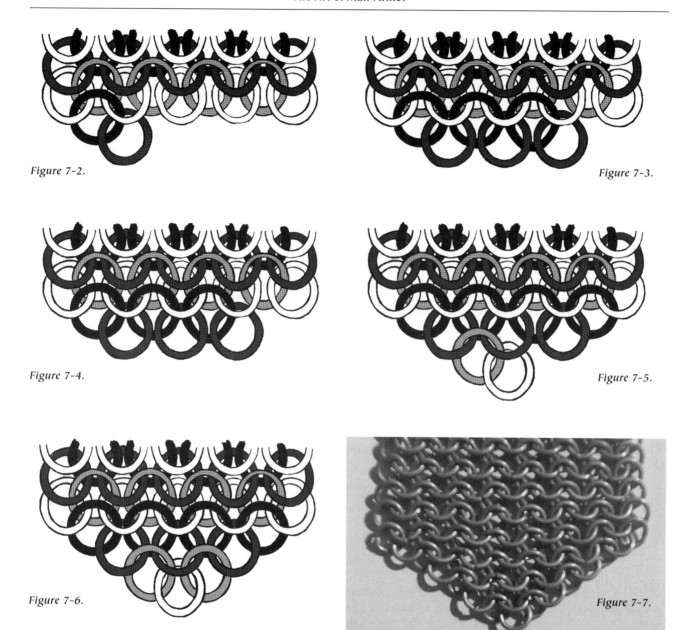

Figure 7-2.

Figure 7-3.

Figure 7-4.

Figure 7-5.

Figure 7-6.

Figure 7-7.

ring on the open ring. The open ring is attached, as usual, through links in columns one and three (Figure 7-2).

The next links are added in the normal manner until you reach the last one in the row (Figure 7-3).

This last open link that you add to the row will have no open ring on it (Figure 7-4).

The next row starts the same as the previous one. You use an open link with only one closed link on it instead of two (Figure 7-5).

Figure 7-6 shows the end open link added to this row and finishing the pattern. The closed link of the last step forms the final point at the tip of the piece. Naturally, there could be many more rows in between rows 1 and 3 that would all be done in the same manner, each one starting the row with only one closed link on an open link and ending with an open link with no closed link on it.

Because drawings look quite different than actual mail, I have included a picture of mail made coming to a point (Figure 7-7).

POINTS—ACROSS

Points can also be made going across or on the sides of the mail. First, start with a piece of mail that you wish to narrow. In this case, you add one open link with one closed link on it to row 1. Normally, you would use two closed links if you were extending the row (Figure 7-8).

Now, you are going to work down those columns. Go to the next row and add one open link with one closed link on it (Figure 7-9).

Continue this until you reach the last row, where you wish it to start tapering upward. At this point you use an open ring without a closed ring on it (the last black ring in Figure 7-10).

Figure 7-11 shows the next two columns added in the same manner as the ones done in Figure 7-8. You place one open ring with one closed ring on it in row 2. Continue in the same manner as you did in Figure 7-9. Remember that you do not add a closed link to the last open link you add.

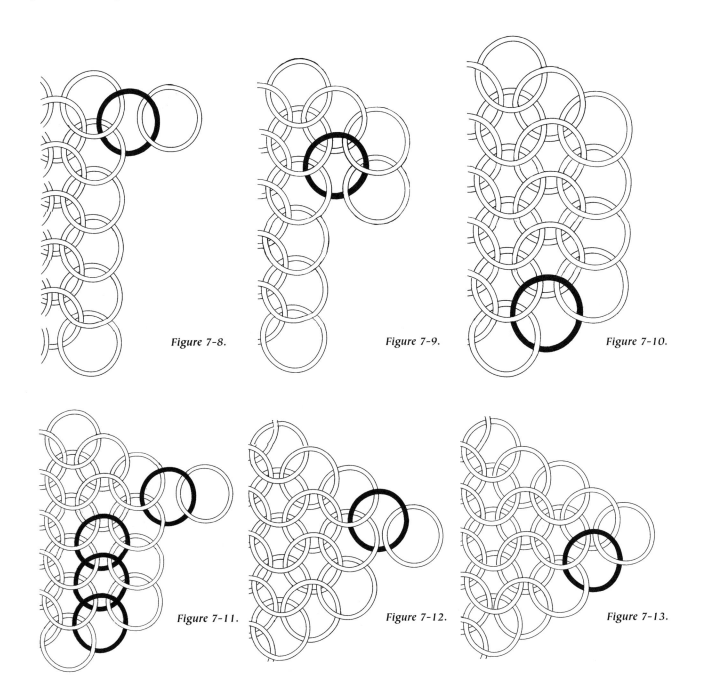

Figure 7-8.

Figure 7-9.

Figure 7-10.

Figure 7-11.

Figure 7-12.

Figure 7-13.

In Figure 7-12 we see the first links added to the next columns, in the same manner that was done in Figures 7-8 and 7-11.

Figure 7-13 shows the next open link (black), which is also the last link of that column, being added to the mail. There is no open link on it. This ring finishes the point.

Figure 7-13A is a photograph of actual mail coming to a sideways point.

ROUNDING

At first this may seem to be an odd addition to this chapter. The reason I include it here with the point section is because the points and rounding are done the same way.

You use the rounding method in many places, such as around the neck in a shirt and the lower face in the aventail of the coif. The procedure is very simple—just remember that you are simply rounding out the corners.

Start where the mail is at a right angle (Figure 7-14).

Next add the black ring (Figure 7-15). The black ring goes through the fourth and then he third ring of the end column, directly below the right angle.

This is the basic idea. By adding a single end ring you round the corner, the same as you do in the bottom section when making a sideways point.

If you wish to have the area even more rounded, which you usually do, simply add another layer of rings. To do this you add a closed ring to a black ring you already added in Figure 7-15. In other words, you would do the same as if you were extending the next row (see Figure 7-16).

Next you add a single open ring in the third column of the addition

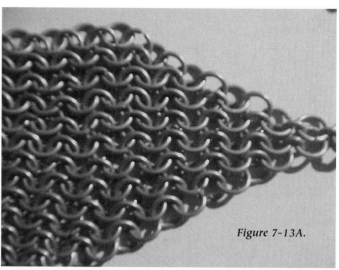

Figure 7-13A.

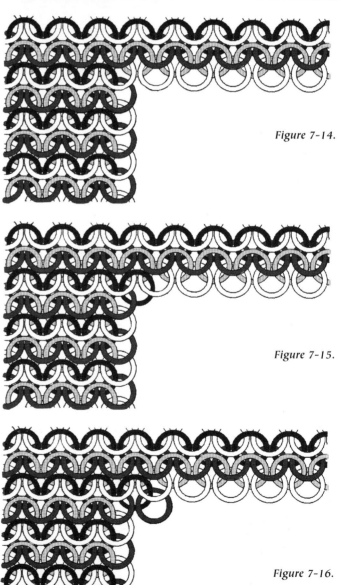

Figure 7-14.

Figure 7-15.

Figure 7-16.

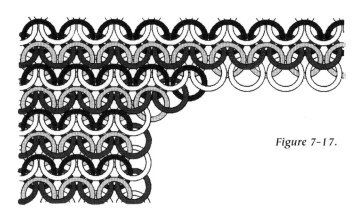

Figure 7-17.

and another single open ring in the first column in the next row (Figure 7-17).

To continue the idea, you can extend the first row as long as you want the curve and then fill in the following rows, stopping one addition short on each row (Figure 7-18).

Then you can fill in the single rings at the end of each row (Figure 7-19 shows a completed curve).

With a little practice you should be able to round and shape to any form you want.

Figure 7-18.

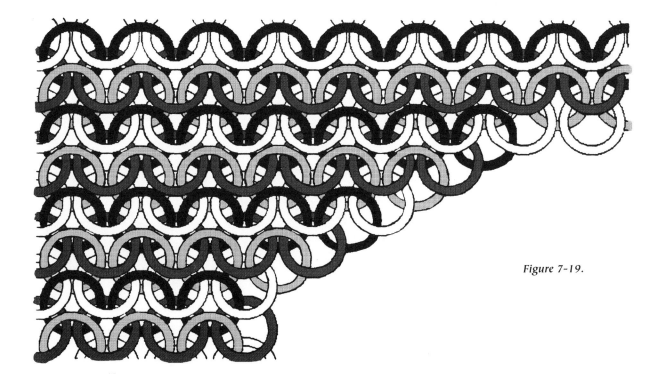

Figure 7-19.

CHAPTER 8

Flairs

What is a flair? It's the term I use for an increase in links to make a piece of mail larger on one side than the other. For example, to make a bishop's collar the mail must sit close to the neck yet spread out to cover the shoulders. If you make it without a flair it will bunch up around the neck and be stretched too tight on the edge. An alternative method is to make four triangular pieces of mail and insert them at both sides and the middle of the front and back.

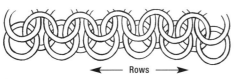

Figure 8-1.

Flairs can be made into what I call "full flairs," where they increase by one row every other column, or "partial flairs," where they increase gradually by one row every second, third, forth, fifth, etc., column.

Figure 8-1 shows starting at a standard row of mail.

In Figure 8-2, when you add the first links of the row, take one open link, place on it three closed links, and go through the bottom link of

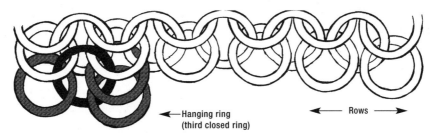

Hanging ring
(third closed ring)

Rows

Figure 8-2.

Figure 8-3.   Hanging ring

column 1 and the bottom link of column 3. This is the same step you use in starting any new row, except that you are placing on three closed links instead of the usual two.

As in Figure 8-3, take one open link, place on one closed link, go through the second and third links of column 3 (not the fourth link of column 3 labeled hanging ring) and the bottom link of column 5. These are shown as black rings in Figure 8-3.

Finish the row from there as you normally would. This is shown in Figure 8-3 as gray rings. Take one open link, add one closed link, go up through the bottom two rings in column 5 and the bottom link of column 7, etc. This will leave that one extra link in column 3 hanging down.

This link will be the start of a new extra row. This is how the "flair" increases, by adding an extra row every other column.

Take one open link and put it on two closed links. Connect to the bottom two links

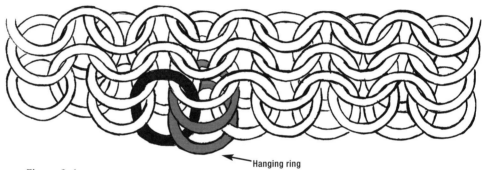

Figure 8-4.   Hanging ring

of column 3 (the bottom one of which is that hanging link just mentioned) and the bottom link of column five (Figure 8-4). Notice that this is like continuing a row except that you use two closed links instead of one. This will again give you a hanging link and a start for an extra row.

Next, take one open link, put on one closed link, connect with the third and fourth rings (not the fifth ring) in column 5 and the bottom ring in column 7. Finish the row as usual

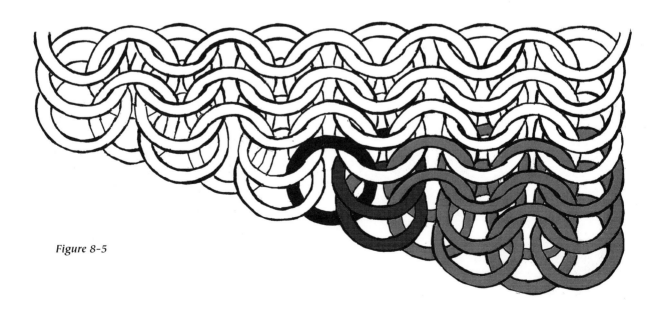

Figure 8-5

(i.e., next, open ring, with one closed ring, connected to bottom two rings, column 7, and the bottom ring, column 9).

Figure 8-5 shows how to take one open ring, put on two closed rings, and connect to bottom two rings in column 5 and the bottom ring in column 7. Here you are again continuing the new row you are inserting and also providing for the start of the next new row. By now you should have the hang of it. Finish the row. Start the next row the same way, between columns 7 and 9; finish the row. But on the last row, at the edge, do not add

Figure 8-6.

two closed links. Add only one. Of course, the longer your row, the wider the flair.

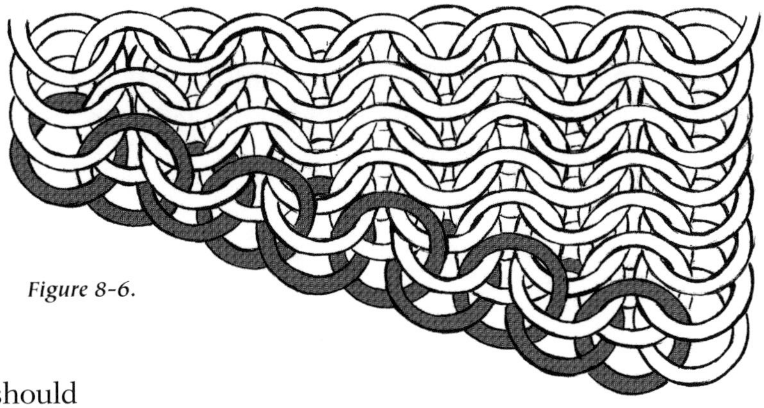

As Figure 8-6 shows, continuing the regular mail pattern is simple. You just do exactly what you have been doing. Start at the left edge with one open link and add two closed links. Go up through the last link in columns 1 and 3. Close the link. Then continue as usual with one closed link on one open link until you reach the end of the row. This drawing shows one row added after the flair.

I have also included a picture of an actual flair (see Figure 8-7). This one was made of 16 1/2-gauge tie wire, which is normally black. I plan on incorporating it into a bishop's collar to be worn as an accessory for fancy dress. Worn over brightly colored cloth or a shiny silver shirt it would look stunning.

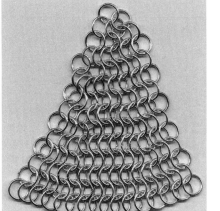

Figure 8-7.

PARTIAL FLAIRS

Figure 8-8 shows a partial flair. The increases are in columns 3 and 7. As you can see, you can add rows at every other column, as in a full flair, or you can skip a column or even two.

A partial flair can be handy under the arms or in collars, among other places. The only difference in this and a full flair is that you do not add that second open ring when you go back to start the new row from your hanging ring. You just add one open ring at that point. But at the next column in which you want an increase, you add the second open ring, giving you a start for a new row to be inserted.

Figure 8-9 is a photograph of a bishop's collar. Notice how it is made with sections, which are flairs.

• • •

To conclude, flairs can be done in either direction by working to

Figure 8-8.

your left instead of your right. Or you can simply turn the mail over and work from the other side. The process is reversible.

A method of working flairs slightly differently is described in the section on making a bishop's mantle at the end of Chapter 15. It is essentially the same, except that more than one flair is done at the same time.

Figure 8-9.

CHAPTER 9

Reductions

ACROSS

Reducing—No, I don't mean dieting and exercising a lot. In the context of mail, reducing is the same as a flair, but in reverse.

As usual you start with the regular mail pattern (left edge). You are going to extend the top row of mail to the left by the same number of columns as you have rows that you wish to reduce, in this case adding six columns to make nine columns across and eight rows down (Figure 9-1).

The next row will be extended to match the first row. Figure 9-2 shows this step.

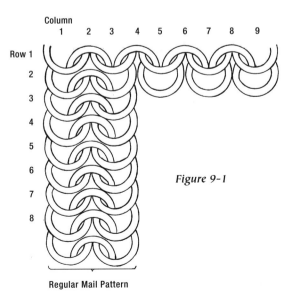

Figure 9-1

Regular Mail Pattern

Figure 9-3 shows the next two rows, 3 and 4, extended across but stopping short one open link from the end of rows 1 and 2, thus ending at column 7.

Figure 9-4 shows the pattern repeated until you reach the left side, leaving the last two rows with no extension, just the original mail. It is simply an upside-down stair step, two columns over and two rows down each time.

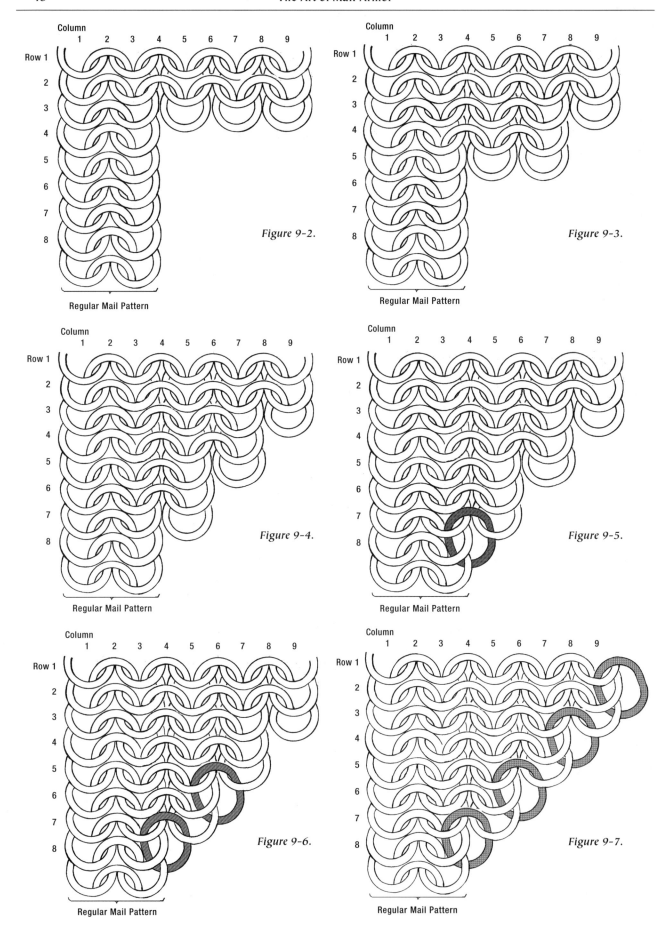

Figure 9-2.

Figure 9-3.

Figure 9-4.

Figure 9-5.

Figure 9-6.

Figure 9-7.

Figure 9-5 shows how to take one open link and go up through the last three rings of column 3 and up through the last two rings of column 5. Close the link. Each end of each "step" will be done in this was to form the reduction. If you look closely at the section on flairs in Chapter 8, you will see that it is the exact opposite.

For Figure 9-6, take an open link and go up through the last three bottom links in column 5 and the bottom two links in column 7.

Figure 9-7 illustrates going up through the last three links in column 7 and the last two links in column 9. It also shows the last open link joining the last three links in column 9. As with a flair, you can simply add the next row down as you normally would.

SIDEWAYS REDUCTIONS

Figure 9-8.

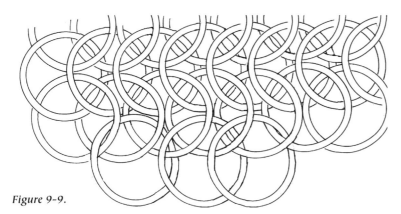

Figure 9-9.

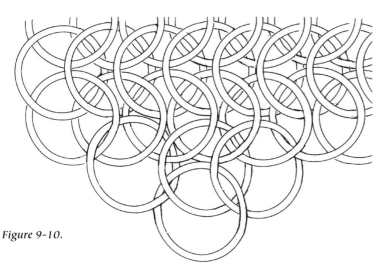

Figure 9-10.

Now we are going to try something a little different. We are going to turn our piece of mail 90 degrees and work on it from the side. At first this might be a little confusing, but just keep the pattern of the mail in mind and you shouldn't have too much trouble. Notice that one link on the end goes through two other links. Figure 9-8 shows this.

To reduce this area, you are just going to go through three links instead of two each time. This will make a very fast reduction. This method is used in the shaping of the top of a coif in the rounded method.

Figure 9-9 shows the open rings going through three rings each. Note that as each open ring picks up three rings it starts with the last ring of the last three picked up.

Figure 9-10 shows the last three rings being gathered by one open ring. For clarity the ring in the drawing is a little larger. In practice, all rings are the same size. This is so simple that I don't think it needs much more explanation.

Figure 9-11 shows a variation on the above. Many times you don't want the reduction to be too drastic too quickly. In that case, you can catch three links together and then go back to the normal pattern of catching only two links for one, two, three (or however

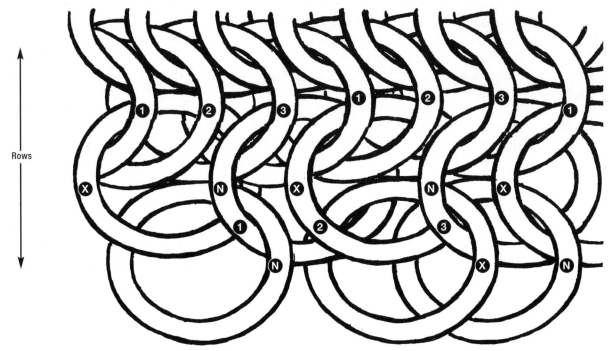

Rows

Figure 9-11.

many you wish) connections and then catch three links again. In the diagram, the links marked X are the ones that catch three links together (each numbered from 1 to 3); those links marked N form the normal pattern connections.

6-on-1 Mail Pattern

Heavier, 6-on-1 mail (each link having six links go through it) is done basically the same as 4-on-1 mail. If you have done your homework and are familiar with the 4-on-1, this will be simple.

The 6-on-1 pattern makes very dense mail. Since there are six links going through every link of the mail, it is necessary to have a bigger inside diameter for the link. The most common size used is 1/2 inch. Along with the increase in the size of the link, it is recommended that you increase the size of the wire to 12-gauge, although 14-gauge can be used. If you try this pattern with 16 1/2-gauge, do not increase the diameter of your links.

Figure 10-1.

Figure 10-1, step one: Start out by placing six closed rings on one open ring and close it. Then place three closed rings on one open ring, thread through three of the original six rings, and close the open ring. So now, you have a chain of 3-1-3-1-3-1-3, as long as you want.

Figure 10-2, step two: Take two closed rings on one open ring, go up through the bottom two rings of column 1 and the bottom two rings of

51

column 3. Yep, just as with 4-on-1 mail, but you pick up two rings in each column instead of one.

Figure 10-3, step three: Put one closed ring on an open ring, up through the bottom three rings of column 3 and the bottom two rings of column 5. Continue to the end of the row.

So, as in the 4-on-1 mail you simply continue the same steps until you have a piece of mail in the size you wish. With a few changes you can also use the techniques for reducing and enlarging the mail.

If you want to make a piece of mail using an 8-on-1 or 10-on-1 design, it is done basically the same way. The main difference is in the number you put on the first chain and how many links up you go in the second row. In the case of 8-on-1 you start with one open link with eight links on it. So, your chain would be 4-1-4-1-4-1-4. When you start your second row, you again use two closed links on one open link and go up through three rings in columns one and three.

NOTE: When you increase the links going through each other, as in six or eight links going through every single link, you have to increase the diameter of the ring also. Otherwise, you won't have room for them to fit through the link.

Figure 10-2.

Figure 10-3.

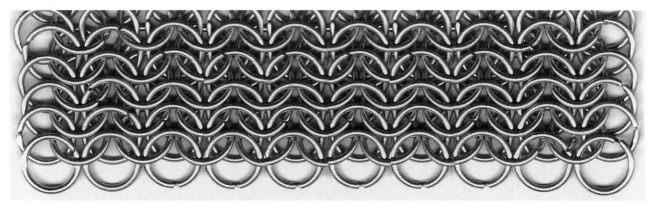

Figure 10-4.

Figure 10-4 is a photograph of a piece of 6-on-1 mail.

CHANGING FROM 4-ON-1 TO 6-ON-1 MAIL

It is easy to join 6-on-1 and 4-on-1 mail for use on edges for trimming, for example. Needless to say, it is much simpler to join them together if they are both of the same diameter and thickness of wire. To join 6-on-1 mail to 4-on-1 mail you simply start your row by going up

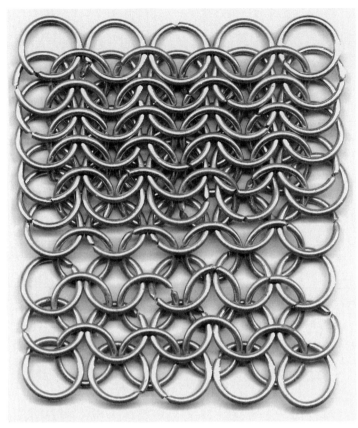

Figure 10-5.

through one link in columns 1 and 3 instead of two links. Continue across the row the same way, going up through one link in each column instead of two links. (If you need, you can refer to the section on joining across in Chapter 5 since it is the same basic process. Just pretend that the 6-on-1 mail is really 4-on-1 mail.)

Be sure that you are thoroughly familiar with the 4-on-1 pattern before you attempt to do the 6-on-1 pattern or join the two patterns together. If you are not adept at the first pattern you will only end up confused and frustrated. Remember also to take it one step at a time. The first time you try it may be confusing, but then things will click and it will seem simple.

To change from 4-on-1 to 6-on-1 mail, you start the row with four closed links on one open link and again go up through the last links in columns 1 and 3. To see an example of this, turn Figure 10-5 upside down.

Continue across the row by adding two closed links on one open link and going up through the last three links in column 3 and the last link in column 5.

In other words, you are doubling the number of closed links you are adding each time. Other than that, it is done exactly the same as you would normally do 4-on-1 mail.

Continue across the row in this manner. For the start of the next row, you take two closed links on one open link; go up through last two links in columns 1 and 3. The next open link will have one closed link on it and go up through the last three links in column 3 and the last two links in column 5.

Figure 10-5 illustrates the two types of mail joined together.

CHAPTER 11

6-on-2
Mail Pattern

Ah, there are a few tricks to this one! This pattern is totally different from the previous ones. It is also a very easy and fast pattern because you don't use the same size of rings. You use two: large closed rings and small open rings. If you use the same size of ring the pattern won't lie correctly, and you won't have the flower-like effect.

As you can see from Figure 11-1, 6-on-2 mail produces a flower-like design. Remember, 4-on-1 mail is so named because each link has four links going through it; 6-on-2 mail has six small links going through two large links, lying on top of each other. The smaller rings stand at right angles to the larger rings, connecting them.

This design makes very heavy mail. It can be used as trimming around edges or, with a little practice, inset into the middle of a piece of mail.

To start out, I suggest you use 14-gauge wire. With the larger rings, use an inside diameter of 1\2 inch. With the smaller rings use an inside

Figure 11-1.

55

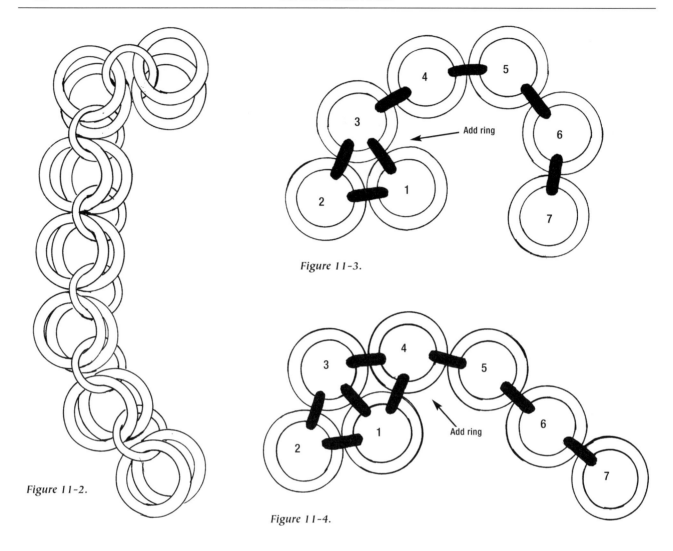

Figure 11-2.

Figure 11-3.

Figure 11-4.

diameter of 3\8 inch. We will start off by making a single flower.

Step 1 (Figure 11-2): As usual we are back to the same basic chain to begin with. The only difference is the alternating sizes of the rings. Your open rings will be small, your closed rings large. Take four large closed rings and place them on one small open link, and close it. Then take two large rings on one small open link and join through two of the previous large closed links, forming a chain of two large, one small, two large, one small, two large. Continue until you have 13 columns, which will be seven pairs of large links with six small links connecting them.

Step 2 (Figure 11-3): Coil the end set of large links of the chain around to touch the third set of links in the chain. The diagram shows only one large link, but remember that there is another link underneath it. Take one

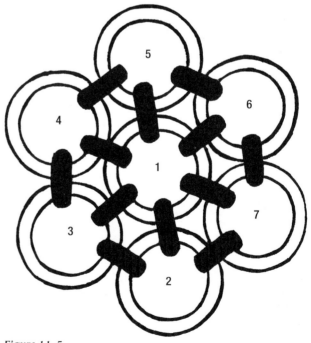

Figure 11-5.

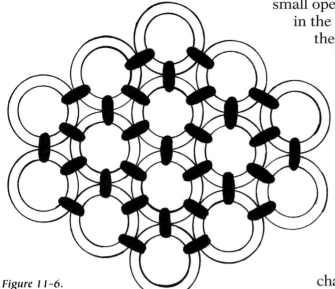

Figure 11-6.

small open link and connect the first two closed links in the chain to the third set of two closed links in the chain. All open links added to make the "flower" will be added through these first two large links of the chain.

Step 3 (Figure 11-4): Again, coil the links a little more. Then take a small open link and connect the two links in the first set of two closed links (yes, the same ones you connected before) with the two closed links in the fourth set of two closed links in your chain.

Continue this with each of the following sets of links in the chain until you have attached the last set of two closed links (number seven) in your original chain to the first two closed links.

Step 4 (Figure 11-5): Take a small open link and go through the two closed links in set seven and the two closed links in set two. You now have one completed flower.

To continue the mail and make the flower design become interlocking and overlapping flowers, you simply make your original chain much longer and continue coiling it around and attaching it to any adjacent pair of rings (Figure 11-6).

I describe this method of doing the 6-on-2 mail first because there are times when it is handier to have a string of flowers, or half flowers, to attach to edges. Another example of the flowers' usefulness is when making some necklaces or hand flowers where you use a flower or triangle shape and connect them together. It is especially handy when you are making new designs. If you have several shapes made, then you can shift them around and get an idea of how they will look when attached.

This design can be used in a number of ways. You can make a whole shirt or coif in this pattern. Another easier way of making this design is to make long chains of 2-1-2-1-2 links, as in Figure 11-2. Make these chains as long as you wish the piece of finished mail to be. Place them side by side and slightly offset. Then simply join the chains together. This method is shown in detail in Chapter 15 under the "Bishop's Mantle or Bishop's Collar" section, complete with diagrams, so I will not detail it here.

Remember that another use for this design is to make a chain of flowers that can be used as edgings around necks, sleeves, bottoms of shirts, or coifs, not to mention bracelets or belts.

Figure 11-7 shows an example of this. You can continue this method to make a chain as long as you wish.

Notice that there is not a connection between links six and eight or between links two and eleven. When making trim that edges a curved piece, such as a

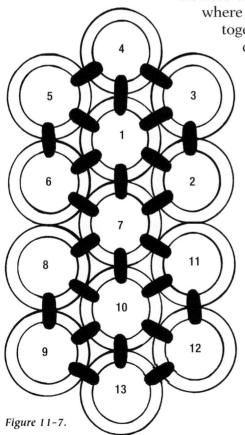

Figure 11-7.

bishop's collar, you might wish to leave these connections missing on the outer side to provide more flexibility or space so your mail will not curl up on the chest.

In other words, you would place a connecting small link between the set of rings labeled 2 and the set of rings labeled 11. This would be the side that would attach to your 4-on-1 mail in a shirt, coif, or bishop's collar. The side with the set of rings labeled 5, 6, 8, and 9 is the edge with no mail attached to it.

In the second flower you attach a continuing chain to set 7. The next set is number 8, the first outer set of the next flower.

Coil sets 9, 10, and 11 around to where set 11 touches set 8; connect sets 11 and 8 and sets 11 and 9.

Coil set 12 to touch set 8 and connect it to set 8. Now reverse direction and coil set 13 to touch set 11. Connect sets 13 and 11.

If you use different types of metal, you can even produce a striped effect. For instance, alternate the rows by using copper rings for the large rings in one row, and the next row use steel for the large rings. Be sure to use at least 12-gauge copper because lower gauges bend too easily and will not hold. Actually, brass welding rods are a better choice than copper wire (Figure 11-8).

Figure 11-8.

There are other ways you can connect these flowers to form chains: see Figure 11-9 for one idea.

Figures 11-10 and 11-11 show some ideas, as well. I use many of these basic patterns in my jewelry designs (see Chapter 20 for photos of these). I'm sure if you try, you can come up with some others.

Figures 11-12 through 11-18 show how to construct a variation of the flower design that I

Figure 11-9.

Figure 11-10.

Figure 11-11.

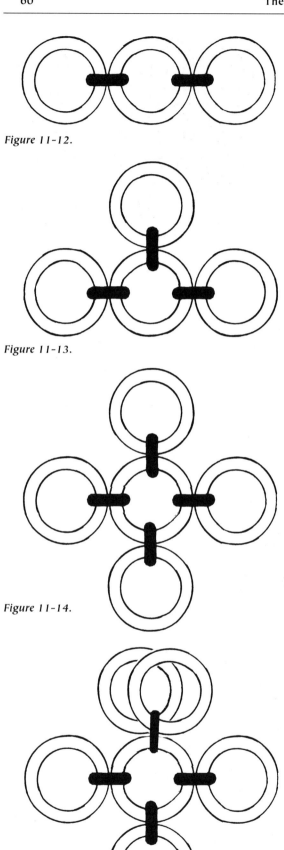

Figure 11-12.

Figure 11-13.

Figure 11-14.

Figure 11-15.

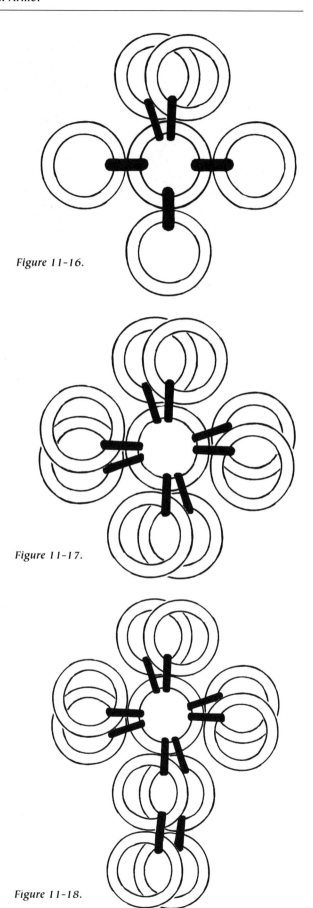

Figure 11-16.

Figure 11-17.

Figure 11-18.

Figure 11-19.

use to make crosses. It is based on the 6-on-2 pattern, but could be called an 8-on-2 pattern.

Start with four large closed links on one small link. Add two large closed links with one small open link to two of the first large links. You now have a chain of two large, one small, two large, one small, two large (Figure 11-12).

Next take two large closed rings on one small open ring and connect them to the middle two large links of your chain (Figure 11-13).

Repeat this step again (Figure 11-14). You now have two large links with four sets of large links connected to it by four small links.

Now use small open rings to separate the outside large links. Gently slide two of the large links of one outside set apart (Figure 11-15).

Insert a small link through the middle two large links and the bottom one of the outside large links. Close (Figure 11-16).

Repeat this step with the other three sets of outside links (Figure 11-17).

To form the bottom of your cross, simply add two large closed links with one small open link to one set of the outside rings. Then separate them in the same way you did the others (Figure 11-18).

Figure 11-19 is an actual picture of one. You will notice that I have added a few more rings to better stabilize it. This takes a little more time and effort, but I think the result is worth it.

When mounted on leather that has been cut in the shape of a shield, these make very nice key chains.

Another variation of the 6-on-2 pattern is the 12-on-2 pattern. This is basically the same pattern, but the rings connecting the large rings are doubled. You can find a more complete description of this pattern in Chapter 19 under the section on 12-on-2 triangular design.

Douglas Archer in Roswell, New Mexico, used this design to create unusual juggling balls. Because they are hollow inside, they are fairly light in weight but perfect for throwing. This one (Figure 11-20) was made of 14-gauge wire in aluminum with a ring size of 3/8-inch inside diameter for the large rings and 1/4-inch inside diameter for the small rings.

The design, similar to a soccer ball, makes them hold their shape exactly. There are 32 sets of large double rings: 12 of these sets are formed of 10-on-2 mail, and 20 sets of 12-on-2 mail. That is to say, if you look at any two sets of large rings, it will be either in the 10-on-2 or 12-on-2 pattern (Figures 11-21 and 11-22).

Figure 11-20.

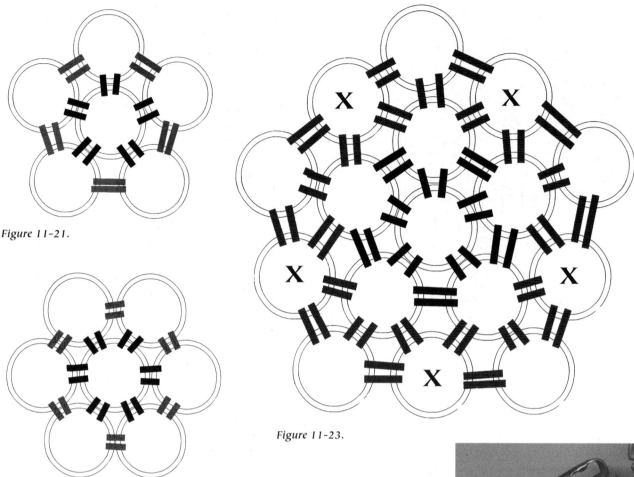

Figure 11-21.

Figure 11-22.

Figure 11-23.

However, the adjoining small rings share the next large rings' pattern. Every cluster of 10-on-2 is surrounded by 12-on-2 clusters (Figure 11-23).

Notice that the center cluster is 10-on-2 (the rings in black), while the surrounding clusters are 12-on-2 (rings in gray and black). All double-ring sets marked with an X are 10-on-2 clusters. The spacing on the diagrams do not match up. Remember that this is a piece that will curve, so in reality the spaces will match.

Douglas also designed earrings made with very tiny rings, using 20-gauge wire in 5/32-inch inside diameter for the large rings and 1/8-inch inside diameter for the small rings. At the edge of the accompanying photo (Figure 11-24) you can see the size of normal mail rings of 3/8 inch. His instructions call for making two 12-on-2 "flowers" first. See Figure 11-22 for a diagram of the 12-on-2 cluster.

Following are the instructions for combining the two clusters, along with a diagram labeling the rings (Figure 11-25).

Links 1 and 14 are on the top and bottom respectively. Join the flowers together in this way:

Figure 11-24.

2 —> 8 and 9 (link 2 to links 8 and 9 with small rings)
3 —> 8 and 13
4 —> 13 and 12
5 —> 12 and 11
6 —> 11 and 10
7 —> 10 and 9

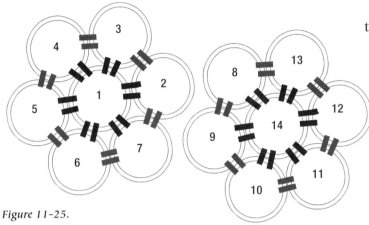

Note that links 1 and 14 are joined in the 12-on-2 pattern and links 2 through 13 are joined in the 10-on-2 pattern.

JOINING 4-ON-1 AND 6-ON-2 OF MAIL

Lay the pieces next to each other, as shown in Figure 11-26 (with your 6-on-2 strip side by side with the 4-on-1 mail.

To connect the two strips use small open links. Take one link and catch the first pair of large links in the first column of the 6-on-2 mail

Figure 11-25.

and then go up through the first two links of the bottom column of the 4-on-1 mail.

The next small open link will go through the second set of large links in the first row of 6-on-2 mail and the third and fourth links of the bottom row of the 4-on-1 mail (Figure 11-27).

Continue linking each next set of large rings in the 6-on-2 mail to the next two links of the 4-on-1 mail until your pieces are joined. Do not go through the same link twice in the 4-on-1 mail. You need the extra spacing for the mail to line up evenly. Remember that mail is flexible, much more so than a drawing, and unfortunately the drawing does not show the alignment as the actual mail will lie.

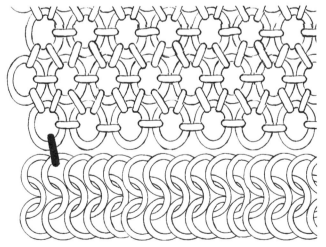

Figure 11-26.

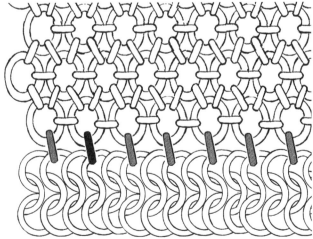

Figure 11-27.

CHAPTER 12

Edge Patterns and Inlaid Designs

EDGE PATTERNS

With a little imagination, you have an almost limitless choice of patterns to use to finish an edge. Not only can you vary the design but also the material. By alternating copper, steel, and other materials you can create a totally different look with the same old pattern.

Figure 12-1 shows some ideas for you to start with. All the patterns are simple variations using reductions, points, and other methods you have already learned, so there isn't much point in repeating them here. I did include some patterns for 6-on-2 mail in these. Both of these patterns can be combined with the 4-on-1 to create even more edgings.

INLAID DESIGNS

One of the most striking things you can do with mail is to inset a design in a different material. If you are using steel, which is silver in color, an inset cross in copper or bronze can be very handsome.

There are a couple of things you have to keep in mind when mixing metals, however. First, some metals react with each other, causing eventual deterioration. To prevent this, I suggest that you coat the mail with varnish. Over time this will wear or discolor, so you will need to remove the old varnish and recoat it. The other problem is the different strengths of metals. Bronze and steel should be no problem in terms of their relative strengths. Bronze is pretty expensive, so I'd recommend using it for just accents. Copper, which is very attractive, is not as strong. You can work around this by using a heavier gauge copper wire.

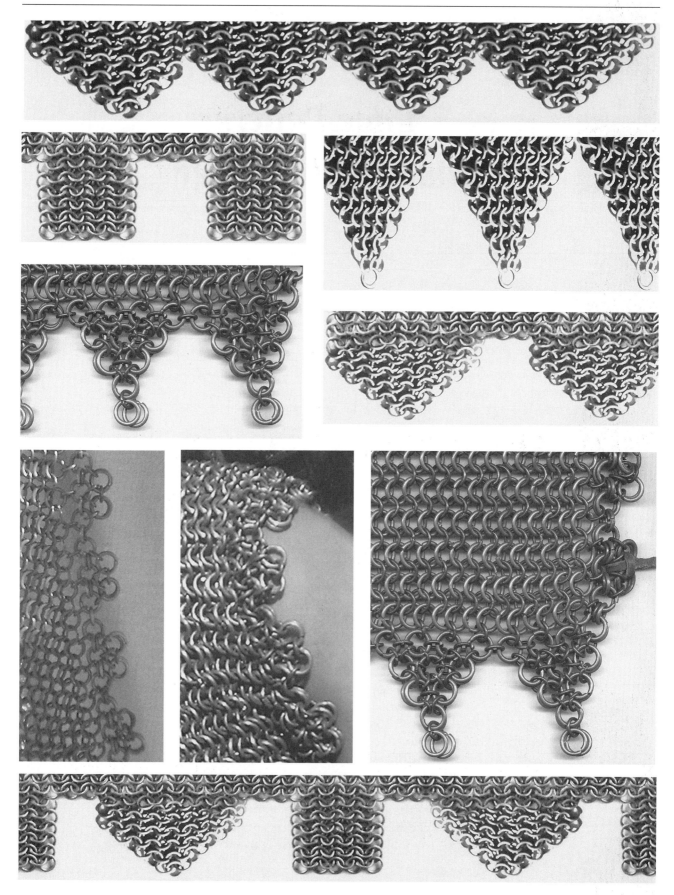

Figure 12-1.

The strength of metal that you need depends on what you are using the mail for. If you are making actual fighting mail, the problem of strength is very important. If you are only planning on wearing it as a costume, strength is not as important.

I have included graphs of four different types of crosses. Since most people will use these as inserts in a shirt, I have made them in fairly large. For such areas as coifs, you can reduce them pretty easily. They can also be used as outline patterns, where the inner portion of the cross returns to the same material as the main body of the mail.

In addition to a graph I have included a chart for each cross. Each chart is made in three columns. The first column covers the left-most area, which is the original material. The center covers the center area, which is the inlay material (for instance brass), and the last column covers the right-most area, which is the original material of the main body of mail. Also, I have noted whether the ring is an open ring being added (o) or a closed ring (c).

If you are doing a cross inset in copper on steel, when the directions give 19 (c) to 21 (c) you use a copper ring for that row in column 19 (c), 20 (o) and 21 (c). Columns 18 and 22 would be steel rings.

Remember, a row consists of rings both open and closed, in alternating directions (Figure 12-2). A column consists of one ring, with all rings in that column going in the same direction (Figure 12-3).

I suggest that you use a twist tie to mark where column one will be. When you reach the area where you want the top of the cross to be, find the center. Measure to the left by half the width of the cross. This will be column 1. Sometimes you will have to skip a column in one direction or the other to line up with an open or closed column. The following row will be row 1.

I also suggest that you mark the center and right sides of the cross with twist ties. Anything that keeps you oriented is helpful, and twist ties are easy to remove.

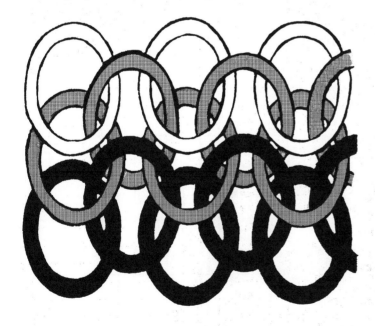

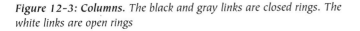
Figure 12-2: Rows.

Figure 12-2: Rows. The black and gray links are each one row. The white links are the edge and do not count as a row. Always count rows from the open ring and the last closed ring added to it.

Figure 12-3: Columns. The black and gray links are closed rings. The white links are open rings

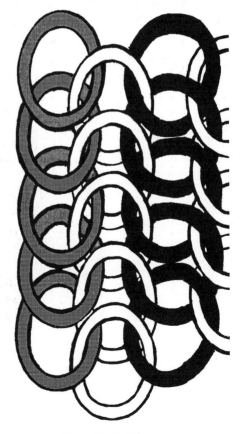
Figure 12-3: Columns.

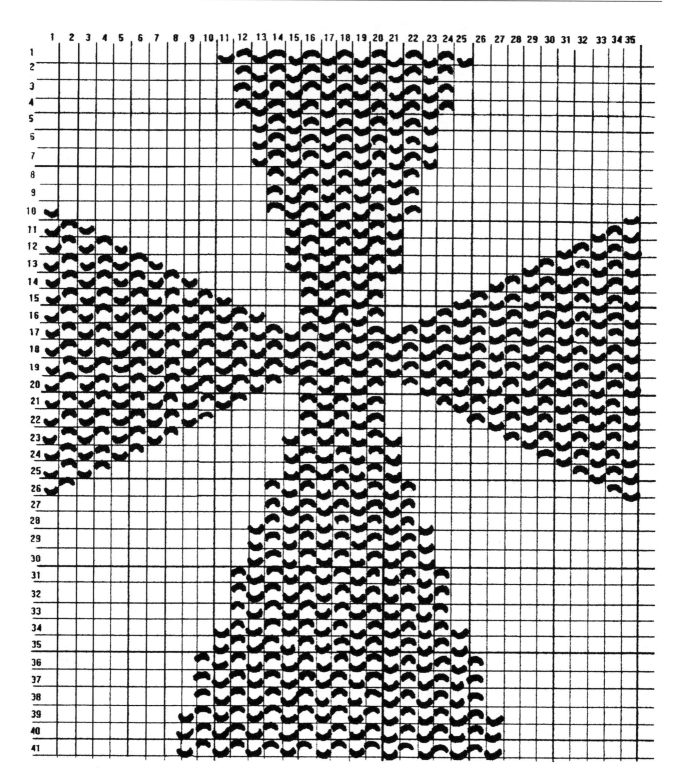

Figure 12-4: Cross number one.

CROSS NUMBER ONE

Cross number one is approximately 12 1/2 inches tall (41 rows) and 10 1/4 inches wide (35 columns). Start by measuring 5 1/8 inches to the left of the center of the top row, where you wish the cross placed. Mark this ring. This will be column one and should be an open ring. The next row will be row 1. The chart below indicates the rings you insert with a *different type of metal* (Figure 12-4).

Remember: A row consists of rings both open (o) and closed (c), alternating directions; a column consists of one ring, with all rings in that column going in the same direction.

ROW	COLUMN
1	11 (o) to 25 (o)
2	12 (c) to 24 (c)
3 and 4	same as row 2
5	13 (o) to 23 (o)
6 and 7	same as row 5
8	14 (c) to 22 (c)
9	same as row 8
10	1 (o) . . . . 14 (c) to 22 (c) . . . . 35 (o)
11	1 (o) to 3 (o) . . . . . 15 (o) to 21 (o) . . . . . . 33 (o) to 35 (o)
12	1 (o) to 5 (o) . . . . . 15 (o) to 21 (o) . . . . . . 31 (o) to 35 (o)
13	1 (o) to 7 (o) . . . . . 15 (o) to 21 (o) . . . . . . 29 (o) to 35 (o)
14	1 (o) to 9 (o) . . . . .16 (c) to 20 (c) . . . . 27 (o) to 35 (o)
15	1 (o) to 11 (o) . . . .16 (c) to 20 (c) . . . . . . .25 (o) to 35 (o)
16	1 (o) to 13 (o) . . . .16 (c) to 20 (c) . . . . . . .23 (o) to 35 (o)
17	1 (o) to 35 (o) cross arm (from one side to the other)
18, 19, and 20	same as 16, cross arm
21	1 (o) to 12 (c) . . . .16 (c) to 20 (c) . . . . .24 (c) to 35 (o)

ROW	COLUMN
22	1 (o) to 10 (c) . . . .16 (c) to 20 (c) . . . . .26 (c) to 35 (o)
23	1 (o) to 8 (c) . . . . .15 (o) to 21 (o) . . . . . . .28 (c) to 35 (o)
24	1 (o) to 6 (c) . . . . .15 (o) to 21 (o) . . . . . . .30 (c) to 35 (o)
25	1 (o) to 4 (c) . . . . .15 (o) to 21 (o) . . . . . . .32 (c) to 35 (o)
26	1 (o) to 2 (c) . . . . .14 (c) to 22 (c) . . . . . . .34 (c) to 35 (o)
27	14 (c) to 22 (c)
28	13 (o) to 23 (o)
29 and 30	same as row 28
31	12 (c) to 24 (c)
32 and 33	same as row 31
34	11 (o) to 25 (o)
35	same as row 34
36	10 (c) to 26 (c)
37 and 38	same as row 36
39	9 (o) to 27 (o)
40 and 41	same as row 39

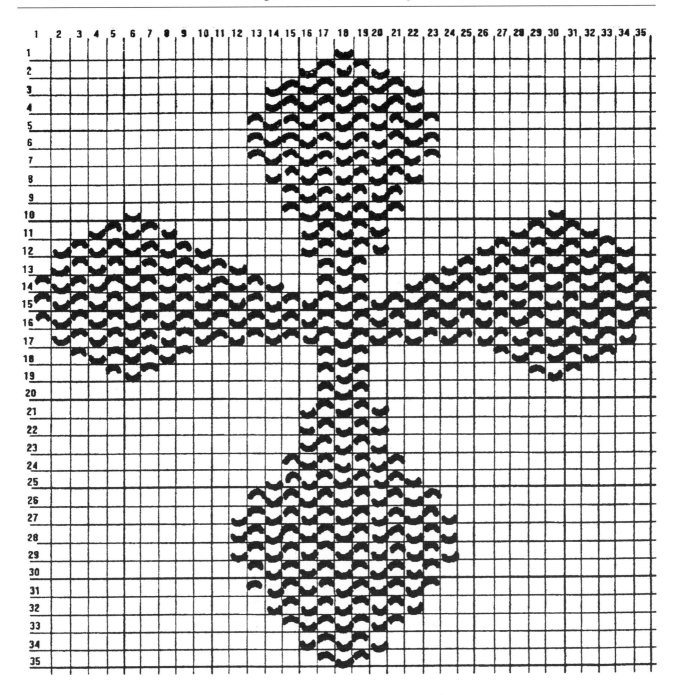

Figure 12-5. Cross number two.

CROSS NUMBER TWO

Cross number two is approximately 10 1/2 inches tall (35 rows) and 10 1/4 inches wide (35 columns). Start by measuring 5 1/8 inches to the left of the center of the top row, where you wish the cross placed. Mark this ring. This will be column 1 and should be a closed ring. The next row will be row 1. Here are the rings you insert with a *different type of metal* (Figure 12-5).

ROW	COLUMN
1	18 (o)
2	16 (o) to 20 (o)
3	14 (o) to 22 (o)
4	same as row 3
5	13 (c) to 23 (c)
6 and 7	same as row 5
8	14 (o) to 22 (o)
9	15 (c) to 21 (c)
10	6 (o) . . . . .15 (c) to 21 (c) . . . . .30 (o)
11	4 (o) to 8 (o) . . . . .16 (o) to 20 (o) . . . . . . .28 (o) to 32 (o)
12	2 (o) to 10 (o) . . . .16 (o) to 20 (o) . . . . . . .26 (o) to 34 (o)
13	2 (o) to 12 (o) . . . .17 (c) to 19 (c) . . . . . . .24 (o) to 34 (o)
14	1 (c) to 14 (c) . . . .17 (c) to 19 (c) . . . . . . .23 (c) to 35 (c)
15 and 16	1 (c) to 35 (c) cross arm and all the way across
17	2 (o) to 34 (o) cross arm
18	3 (c) to 9 (c) . . . . .17 (c) to 19 (c) . . . . . . .27 (c) to 33 (c)
19	5 (c) to 7 (c) . . . . .17 (c) to 19 (c) . . . . . . .29 (c) to 31 (c)
20	17 (c) to 19 (c)
21	16 (o) to 20 (o)
22	same as row 21
23	15 (c) to 21 (c)
24	same as row 23
25	14 (o) to 22 (o)
26	13 (c) to 23 (c)

ROW	COLUMN
27	12 (o) to 24 (o)
28 and 29	same as row 27
30	13 (c) to 23 (c)
31	same as row 30
32	14 (o) to 22 (o)
33	15 (c) to 21 (c)
34	16 (o) to 20 (o)
35	17 (c) to 19 (c)

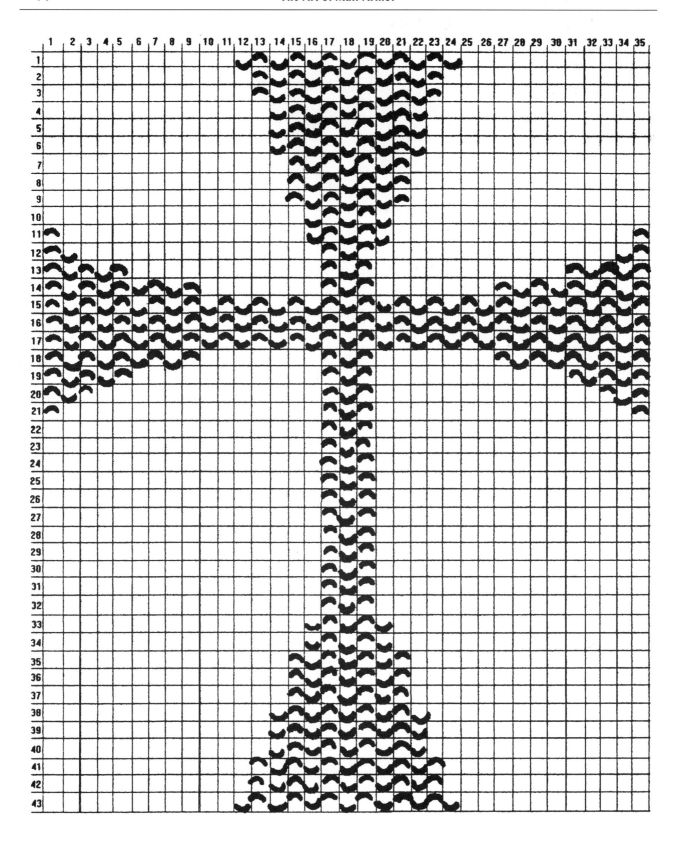

Figure 12-6. Cross number three.

CROSS NUMBER THREE

Cross number three is approximately 14 1/2 inches tall (43 rows) and 10 1/4 inches wide (35 columns). Start by measuring 5 1/8 inches to the left of the center of the top row, where you wish the cross placed. Mark this ring. This will be column one and should be a closed ring. The next row will be row 1e. Here are the rings you insert with a *different type of metal* (Figure 12-6):

ROW	COLUMN
1	12 (o) to 24 (o)
2	13 (c) to 23 (c)
3	same as row 2
4	14 (o) to 22 (o)
5 and 6	same as row 4
7	15 (c) to 21 (c)
8 and 9	same as row 7
10	16 (o) to 20 (o)
11	1 (c) . . . . .16 (o) to 20 (o) . . . . .35 (c)
12	1 (c) to 2 (o) . . . . .17 (c) to 19 (c) . . . . .34 (o) to 35 (c)
13	1 (c) to 5 (c) . . . . .17 (c) to 19 (c) . . . . .31 (c) to 35 (c)
14	1 (c) to 9 (c) . . . . .17 (c) to 19 (c) . . . . .27 (c) to 35 (c)
15, 16, and 17	1 (c) to 35 (o) cross arm (totally across)
18	1 (c) to 9 (c) . . . . .17 (c) to 19 (c) . . . . .27 (c) to 35 (c)
19	1 (c) to 5 (c) . . . . .17 (c) to 19 (c) . . . . .31 (c) to 35 (c)
20	1 (c) to 3 (c) . . . . .17 (c) to 19 (c) . . . . . . .33 (c) to 35 (c)
21	1 (c) . . . . .17 (c) to 19 (c) . . . . .35 (c)
22	17 (c) to 19 (c)
23 to 32	same as row 22
33	16 (o) to 20 (o)

ROW	COLUMN
34	same as row 33
35	15 (c) to 21 (c)
36 and 37	same as row 35
38	14 (o) to 22 (o)
39 and 40	same as row 38
41	13 (c) to 23 (c)
42	same as row 41
43	12 (o) to 24 (o)

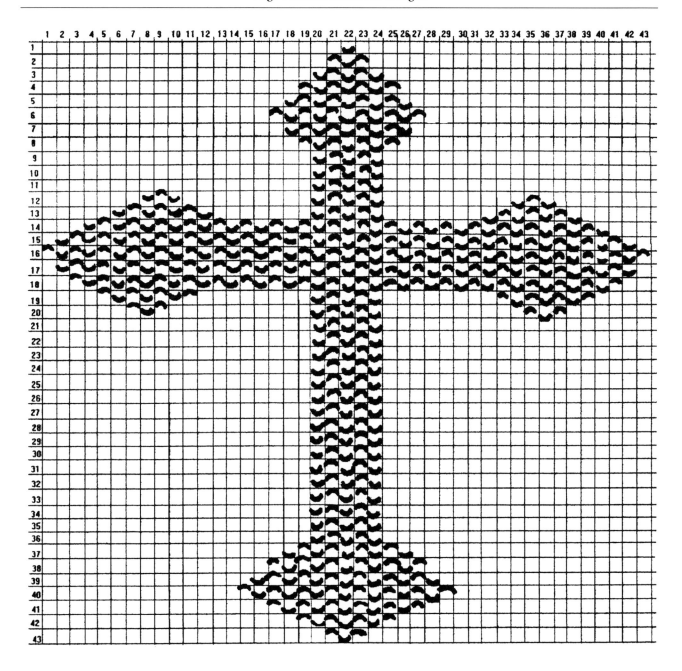

Figure 12-7. Cross number four.

CROSS NUMBER FOUR

To make a cross in the shape of number four, in a size of approximately 15 inches high (43 rows) and 12 inches wide (43 columns), you start by measuring 6 inches to the left from the center of the top and marking that as column 1. The following row is row 1. The first column should be of closed link (Figure 12-7). Here's your pattern:

ROW	COLUMN
1	22 (0)
2	21 (c) to 23 (c)
3	20 (o) to 24 (o)
4	19 (c) to 25 (c)
5	18 (o) to 26 (o)
6	17 (c) to 27 (c)
7	18 (o) to 26 (o)
8	19 (c) to 25 (c)
9	20 (o) to 24 (o)
10 and 11	same as 9
12	8 (o) to 10 (o) . . . .20 (o) to 24 (o) . . . . . . .34 (o) to 36 (o)
13	6 (o) to 12 (o) . . .20 (o) to 24 (o) . . . . . . .32 (o) to 38 (o)
14	4 (o) to 40 (o) cross arm
15	2 (o) to 42 (o) cross arm
16	1 (c) to 43 (c) cross arm—midpoint arm
17	2 (o) to 42 (o) cross arm
18	3 (c) to 41 (c) cross arm
19	5 (c) to 11 (c) . . . .20 (o) to 24 (o) . . . . . . .33 (c) to 39 (c)
20	7 (c) to 9 (c) . . . . .20 (o) to 24 (o) . . . . . . .35 (c) to 37 (c)
21	20 (o) to 24 (o)
22 through 36	same as 21
37	18 (o) to 26 (o)
38	17 (c) to 27 (c)
39	16 (o) to 28 (o)
40	15 (c) to 29 (c)

ROW	COLUMN
41	17 (c) to 27 (c)
42	19 (c) to 25 (c)
43	21 (c) to 23 (c)

All the preceding directions are for adding the cross as you do the mail, and all in one step. There is another way to do this that might be simpler for some people (the charts for each cross can still be used in this method).

You can make the cross first in the color you want for the inset (just the cross). Then you can add links in the other material to fill it out to a square using the techniques you learned in extending in Chapter 6. Once you have the square with the design in it, simply insert it in the piece you are making. This technique is better if you are creating a different design or working in a different style of mail.

Figure 12-8 shows a cross made of 6-on-2 mail and embedded in 4-on-1 mail. Notice that it is attached to the 4-on-1 with small black links. The black rings were made of electric fence wire and coated with black patina, which does not come off. I have tried using bluing and stove black, but it does not work as well.

With steel (but not with galvanized metal), an alternative is to heat the metal until it becomes red, douse it in water, and then boil it in old car oil for an hour or so. Coat hangers turn out very nice this way. This method takes a great deal of time, but it produces a beautiful brownish-black color with red highlights. It also helps to protect against rust. You should know that galvanized metal turns yellow and gives off toxic fumes when heated.

Another method of inlaying designs is shown in Chapter 19 under the double 4-on-1 pattern. Because it is covered there, I do not go into this method in this chapter.

Figure 12-8.

CHAPTER 13

Shirt or Hauberk

There are all kinds of ways to make a shirt. You can make a single long chain that goes all the way around in a circle and knit it upward, coming to the shoulders and then adding arms. Or just go up the front and down the back with an extension out for the arms and a hole in the center for the neck. But these methods might lead you into difficulties.

Generally, shirts are made like a T-shirt, which you just slip over your head. A slit in the front is necessary to allow the head to pass through. This is generally fastened together by leather thongs, which are attached to the rings on either side.

Before you begin you will need measurements of the person who is to wear the hauberk:

- Width of the neck.
- Width from neck to point of shoulder.
- Thickness of the neck from front to back.
- Thickness of the neck from side to side.
- Width of shoulders: Measure both across the back of the neck and across the front of the neck).
- Width of side: From where the front meets the side, to the point where the back meets the side, the underarm area.
- Arm area: From the point of the shoulder down to a point 2 inches below the level of the armpit and back up to point of the shoulder. The easiest way to do this is to loop a heavy string or cord over your shoulder and around under the arm, and then to measure the length of the string.

- Top arm: From the point halfway between the top of arm and beginning of the armpit area—where the side will join the front or back—to an equal place on other side of the arm (refer to Figure 13-1, the X on each side of the diagram).
- Circumference of the chest, below the arms.
- Circumference of the arm at the largest upper part.
- Circumference of the arm at the elbow area (allow for movement of the arm to bend).
- Circumference of the largest part of the lower arm if making long sleeves.
- Length of the sleeves. This should include references for the elbow area.
- Circumference of the waist.
- Circumference of the hips.
- Length from midshoulder to waist.
- Length form waist to midthigh (or desired length).

Step 1: I recommend starting with the neck area first. This allows you to fit it around the neck without 30 pounds of metal hanging down. So, first make a square piece of mail about 6 inches deep and the width of the shoulders (refer to Figure 13-1).

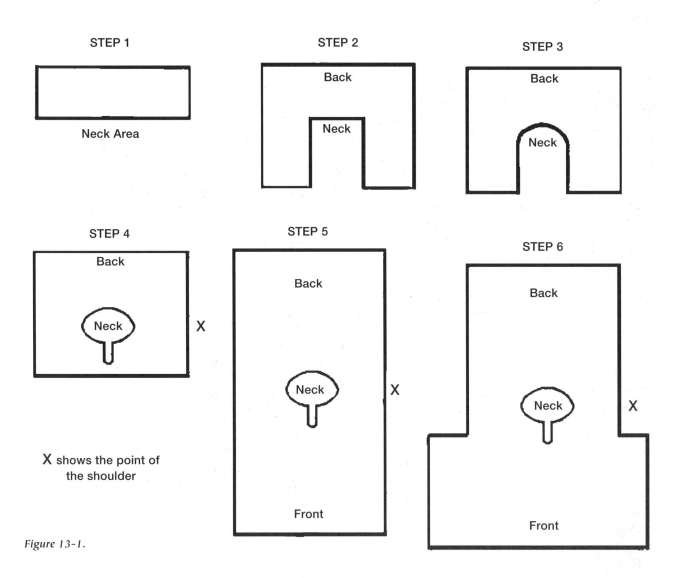

Figure 13-1.

Step 2: Next add strips to both sides to form the top of the shoulders. These should start at both edges and go in width from the neck to the point of the shoulder. When you took this measurement, you should not have run up over the neck. If you did, make it a little shorter (see step 2 in Figure 13-1). Continue these strips to about 10 or 12 inches.

Step 3: This shows the next section going across to join the two strips in the front, but with a slit left in the middle. Start going across at a point on the inside of the first strip and down from the back portion by the thickness of the neck area. Simply extend each side half the distance of the width of the neck and work down for about 3 inches. From there work the rows all the way across, joining the two halves together. Actually, after the first row is joined, it isn't a bad idea to try this over the head to make sure it goes on easily. If it does, continue down, adding rows until you have at least several inches below the slit.

Step 4: Now trim the area around the neck by adding rings in the corners to gradually round the neck area and make it lie closely around the neck. How to do this is covered in Chapter 7, in the section on rounding. This should now fit neatly and come to the point of the shoulder on each side.

Steps 5 and 6: Extend the front and back of the shirt down about 3 inches below the armpit. Next, extend the sides of the front to make the sides that will go under the arm. The side extensions should start 2 inches below the armpit area. You don't want the arm to dig in, and you need some space to allow for movement. At this point, the width of the back plus the width of the front with the side additions should equal the circumference of the chest.

Join the sides to the back of the shirt. Again, after the first row or two is joined, it might be a good idea to try it on. Then if you need to increase or decrease the size, you won't have much to remove. If everything fits fine, join the sides completely.

At this point you should have a vest-like garment that comes to about the bottom of the ribs. Continue your mail down and all around until you reach the top of the leg. Remember that you need to form a slit at the front and back from this point. Simply start at the middle of the front, and work to the middle of the back. Then, start again at the middle of the back and work to the middle of the front, not joining the two rings at either middle.

Now we come to the hard part, the sleeves. Look at the sleeve of a T-shirt. It is not simply a round tubelike extension to the side. It loops up at the top, taller and longer at that point than at the underside of the arm. We have to do the same with mail to make the sleeve fit properly. With mail it is a little more difficult because it doesn't have as much give and is considerably thicker. You want it to lie smoothly on the arm when the arm is down, not bunch up, but you also need to allow the arm to move without binding.

The arm will be made separately and then attached to the armhole. But first you must prepare the armholes. Take a look at Figure 13-2. This shows the direction that the mail will lie in from a side view of the arm. Notice that the mail at the top of the arm has the rows continuing straight down the arm. You might also look at the pictures of the mail from the museums found in the photo gallery at the end of this book.

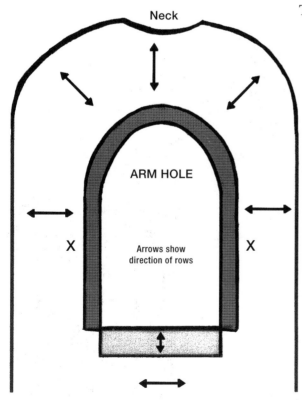

Neck

ARM HOLE

X   X

Arrows show
direction of rows

Figure 13-2.

The problem is that the mail on the underside of the arm goes at right angles to the mail in the main shirt body. You need to make a piece to be added to the top of the side, directly below the armpit, attach it at right angles, and then attach it to the side of the chest in such a way that all the rows will continue down the arm.

The gray shaded areas in figure 13-2 are the ones you added next. The X on each side marks the spot you will measure from for the mail to go straight down without a reduction. Make a piece of mail seven columns wide with the length the same as the width of the area under the arm. This is the side extension that you made from the front of the shirt and attached to the back. You attach this piece to the underarm area at right angles so that the rows going across are attached to the columns you just made (refer to Chapter 5, "At Right Angles," to see how this is done).

Next you add an extension around the rest of the arm. Starting at one corner of the underarm area, add 2 columns all around the area for the upper arm. The reason for this is that the upper arm at the point of the shoulder sticks out farther than the lower arm. Also, you need these rows to turn and attach the mail you just added at the bottom of the arm.

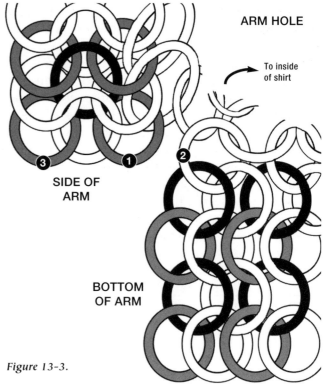

Figure 13-3.

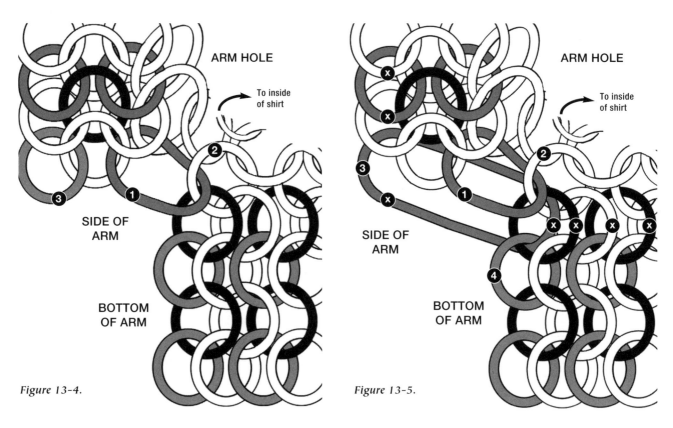

Figure 13-4.

Figure 13-5.

This looks a lot more complicated than it is. Just take it a step at a time. Figure 13-3 shows you the corner of the arm area where the side meets the underarm area. Because the mail at this point curves down into the shirt, it is very difficult to draw properly. The arm hole area goes to the inside of the shirt. The area labeled "bottom of arm" is the piece you added at right angles to the underarm area. The white and gray rings directly below the arm hole area are the ones that join the pieces at right angles. The area labeled "side of arm" contains the columns you added around the upper-arm area.

Figure 13-4 shows the first step in connecting these pieces. Take the link labeled 1 and open it. Slide it under the link labeled 2 and close it again. Some people do not like to reopen links, but at times it makes a complicated section a great deal easier to work.

Link 1 is drawn in an elongated fashion here for the sake of clarity. In reality it remains round and the same size as the other links. As I have mentioned elsewhere, real mail moves and bends, but drawings on paper do not.

Figure 13-5 again uses an elongated link in the drawing, although the link is the same size as the others. This shows the link labeled 3 opened and placed through the links labeled 2 and 4. As you pull the mail together with your link, it will fit smoothly.

In the drawing you will also notice some links marked with an X. One of them is the link numbered 3. If you look closely you will see that these links form a column all the way from the bottom, around the corner, and up along the top of the arm. You have managed to turn your corner.

Now you have to do the same thing to the other side of the arm, where the side meets the underarm. When you have finished this, you should have a column that goes smoothly all around the whole arm area. You will have a couple of extra columns at the bottom of the arm area.

Next you have to make the arm that attaches to this. To start, make a piece of mail 16 rows wide and about 9 inches long. Remember that measurement you took around the arm from halfway down the shoulder, across the top, and halfway down the back? Measure your rows and see whether they are this size. If not, add to them until they reach that measurement. This is the top of your arm and is attached directly to the mail at the point of the shoulder. So, get out a twist tie and mark the middle ring. This lines up with the point of the shoulder that you marked on your shirt. Don't attach it yet.

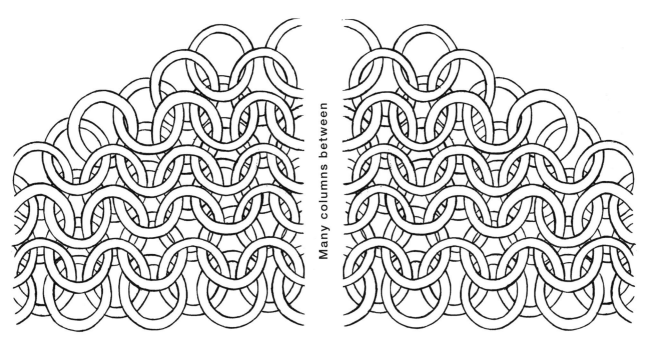

Figure 13-6.

As I said before, an arm is not just a straight extension of the mail. I have seen them made this way, but they tend to bunch up toward the front and rear side of the arm. For a better fit here, I like to put in a slight reduction from the mid-point of the side of the arm to the armpit area.

To do this, use the same method that you use to make points (explained in Chapter 7). From the top of the arm, I start the next row two columns in from the end. The next row is done the same way, started two columns in from the end of the previous row, making a stairstep. This is done on both sides of the mail that forms the middle outside of the arm, until you reach a length equal to the beginning of the underarm, where those extra columns are on your shirt (Figure 13-6).

Next, attach the sleeve to the shirt even though the sleeve is not completely finished (it still lacks the bottom of the arm area). I find it much easier to attach it at this point and then fill in the bottom. That way you have access to both sides of the mail and are not trying to work through a small hole.

Line up the straight top piece of the arm by your twist ties to the middle of the armhole. Start by attaching it here and then working downward until you come to the reduced area. Go back up to the top and work in the other direction, attaching the sleeve to the shirt down till you reach the reduced area again.

The reduced area is attached to the shirt by the method explained in Chapter 5, "At a Slant." Again, taking one side of the arm at a time, join these areas to the shirt. When you are done you should have a short sleeve, except for the bottom. This is a good time to try on the garment to make sure that the fit is comfortable.

It's almost done! All that remains is to fill in the bottom of the arm area. For the first several inches just extend the rows, connecting to the areas already done. As you reach the elbow area you will want to reduce the circumference. This is best done on the bottom of the arm where it cannot be readily seen (see the sideways reduction method described in Chapter 9). Do not make the reduction very drastic. Actually, I suggest that you extend the top of the arms 10 rows to the length that you wish and fill in the bottom with the reduction method as you go along.

Next, make the other arm the same way. That's it. You have a hauberk (Figures 13-7 and 13-8). Now you need a coif and some gauntlets to go with it. On to the next challenge!

Figure 13-7.

Figure 13-8.

VEST

A variation of the shirt is the vest. It is much simpler to make than a shirt because you do not have to make and fit sleeves. Figures 13-09 and 13-10 show a vest modeled by Raven.

The basic pattern is done the same as the first part of the shirt. The next three pictures (Figures 13-11 through 13-13) show the design of the edges for the above vest. (For greater detail refer to Chapter 12.)

Here's a last interesting idea for the vest. You can make epaulets to fit over the top of the

arm area that can be detached, something to clip on and hang over the arm even as low as the elbow area. The vest can be worn with or without the epaulets, giving it two distinct looks. Also, it's a lot easier than fitting in sleeves.

I suggest that you make the epaulets from the bottom of the armpit, over the shoulder, to the back to the armpit area. I would not reduce them. Adding trim along this area adds a more finished and ornamental look. Remember, you must allow for the movement of the arm.

Figure 13-9.   *Figure 13-10.*

Figure 13-12.

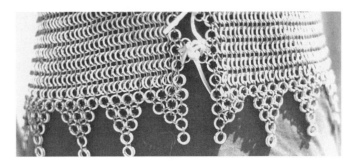

Figure 13-11.   *Figure 13-13.*

CHAPTER 14

Coif—Round Method

There are several ways to make coifs. The most common seems to be the round method. Just for the record, I think this is the most difficult way to make a coif. The other two methods described at the end of this chapter and in Chapter 15 are much easier.

The round method starts with a single open ring with from six to eight closed rings on it. You work sideways to the usual method. In other words, the columns will go across, and the rows will go up and down. Look at Figure 14-2—starting with the two rings in the lower left-hand corner and going toward the center, you will see a 2-1-2 pattern.

As in Figure 14-1, place six closed links on one open link and close the link. This is the crown of your coif.

Place two closed links on one open link and connect through two of the six previous closed links, as shown in Figure 14-2

As in Figure 14-3, you place similar sets of links all around the original set of six closed links, but each time you go through one of the six links that you just connected, and one more of the six links of the original set. So, take two closed links on one open link, and connect to the last one of the six links in the original set that you connected to before and the next

Figure 14-1.

link of the six. Continue this around until
you join with the first link of the six that
you used. *It is extremely important that your
links face the right directions*, or you will
become totally confused!

   You now have (1) a center ring with six
rings on it, (2) in the next column, six rings
attached to the other six rings, and (3) in
the next column, 12 rings around. Or
columns of 1, 6, 6, 12. But you don't want
that—you want columns of 1, 6, 12, 18.

   "Rats!" you say. "Do I have to start
over?" No. Now we pull a sneaky. Pay
close attention!

   As in Figure 14-4, take an open ring. Put
one closed ring on it and connect to just

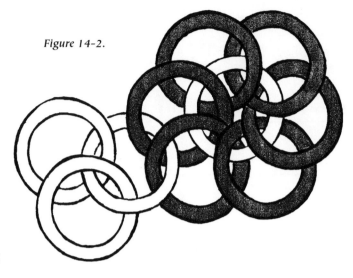

Figure 14-2.

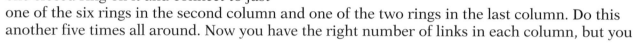

one of the six rings in the second column and one of the two rings in the last column. Do this
another five times all around. Now you have the right number of links in each column, but you

Figure 14-3.

have a few gaps. Next, open ring A and slip on ring B and close ring A again. Do this all around.

Some people hate to open a link once it has been closed, and I agree with them. However, there are times when it seems faster and easier. You can do this pattern by adding one link at a time, but I find that pretty slow. To me it is less confusing and much faster to reopen the links. After all, there are only six of them.

You will notice that this has a rather hexagonal (six-sided) shape. From here you can continue in the same manner, adding extra links every other or every third set . . . or you can turn it sideways and start working like you normally do using a "flair" technique for the next five to ten rows. Keep trying it on your head until it suits you. Don't forget to allow for padding underneath, as the mail will definitely be more comfortable that way, especially if you get hit on the head. Once you reach the area where your head starts to slope back toward your neck, it is a matter of lengthening the sides and back to the neck area and possibly adding a collar.

Figure 14-4.

ANOTHER COIF IDEA

Another way to make a coif is to start with a piece of mail that is 4 or 5 inches deep and goes from one side of the face around the head to the other side. This would form the part of the coif that is near the ears (Figure 14-5).

Next, add another row on the end, about seven columns wide. Continue adding these rows until you reach a length to fit across the top of the head and connect to the other side.

Then round the inside corner areas a little. This is similar in shape to the outside edge of the bowl, with the inside missing.

You then work upward to the top of the head in a circular pattern, gradually gathering the mail in by the reductions method.

Instead of picking up two links, you would pick up three. This isn't done with every stitch, but at first maybe every fourth, then in a few rows every third, until you can combine the remaining links onto one link, in a way very similar to the previous method, and much easier and less confusing.

As with the other method, be sure to keep checking the fit. Mail does have a certain amount of give, but you don't

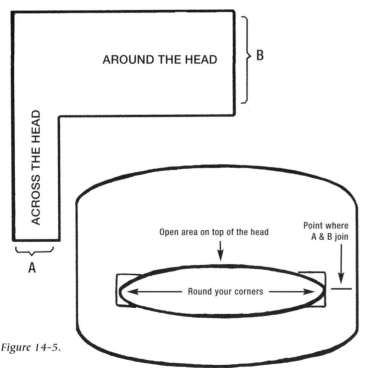

Figure 14-5.

want it to become bunched up in a knot on your head.

Also, you might find it more practical to use a larger size ring for the last gather at the top. With six rings going through one ring, it does become a little crowded, and with a larger ring it will lie flatter.

If, with the gathering, the coif does not come close enough to the face, you can simply add rows to it. Once you have the top done you can extend the sides and back to the desired length or add a bishop's collar.

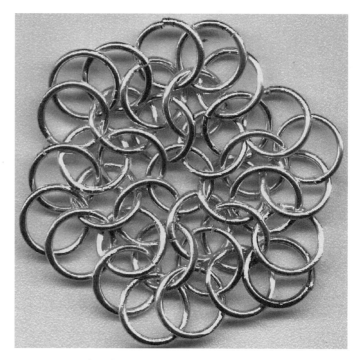

Figure 14-6. This photo shows the start of a round coif.

CHAPTER 15

Coif with Bishop's Collar—
Square Construction

This is the easiest and least confusing method I have found to construct a coif. These are basic measurements for a medium coif to be worn with little padding. If you plan on using heavy padding or have a large head, use the measurements shown in parentheses. Then simply add columns around the face area when the main portion of the coif is done to make some adjustment for size.

As in Figure 15-1, first make a chain 13 (15) inches long. This chain will form the D and E section at the top of the diagram. (The aventail and bishop's collar will be added later.) Continue working this chain until it forms a rectangle of mail the 13 (15) by 8 inches. In other words, add rows until you reach an 8-inch length down.

The next row starts 4 inches in from the left side and goes all the way across the rest of the chain. Continue adding rows until you have added 12 inches down. You will have an L-shaped piece of mail 13 (15) inches across and 20 inches long on the right side. This will be "folded" over to form the crown of the coif.

Now comes the tricky part. Part A must be joined to part a, and part B joined to part b. Fold the mail over into place and look. You will see something neat. Yes, the rows and columns all match up, except at the crown of the head. To join them pull part A around until it is lying parallel to part a.

Study Figure 15-2. It is drawn lying flat because I have yet to figure out how to do a three-dimensional drawing of this. Spot your pivot ring. This is the end ring that your corner will "turn" on.

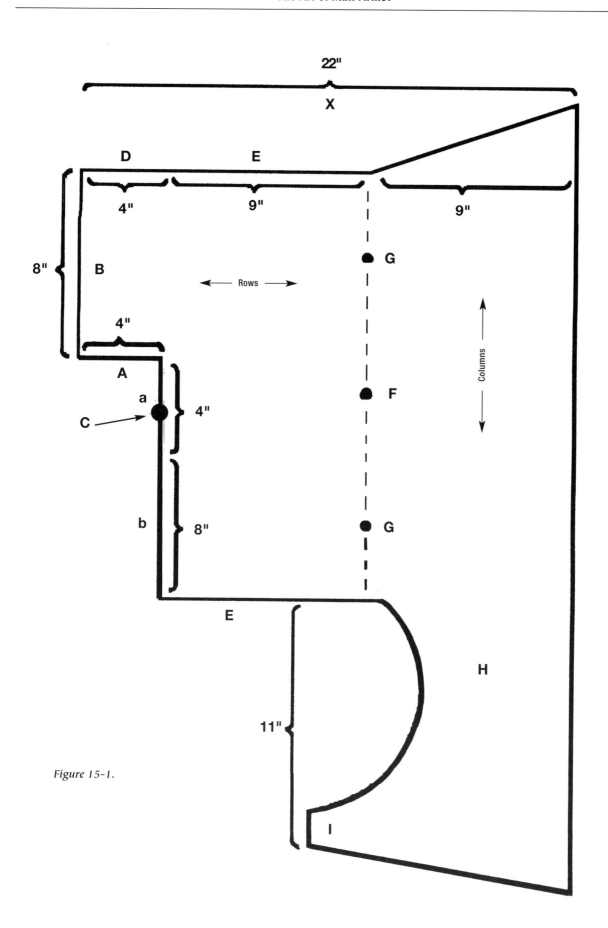

Figure 15-1.

Open ring B and slide it on ring A. Close ring B.

Open ring C and slide on the pivot ring and ring B. Close ring C. You are going to ask, "Why can't I just open ring C and slide on ring A and ring B?" Simple, you first have to get rings A and B connected or you will have a lump.

Next open ring D and slide on rings E and F.

A pattern has been established here. Continue by taking the next ring, slanting up in the side and connecting to the next two rings in the top until you reach the end of the side, *except for the last ring*. This ring should *go through four top rings*, as shown in Figure 15-3.

Lying flat, this might look a little bunchy. Trust me, it fits the top of the head beautifully.

Now for the second corner. Find the on the right in Figure 15-3. That's the row that you just connected across, ending with four rings on the last side ring. This ring becomes your pivot ring for this corner.

Open ring A and add rings B and C. Close ring A.

Next open ring D and add rings E and B. Close ring D.

Now open ring F and add rings G and E.

Again, we have established a pattern. Continue this until you reach the end of the mail.

The top of your coif should be complete now except for the trim around the face. This makes a short neck-length coif at this point. You can adjust it easily to any length you wish. However, I prefer to continue the coif into a bishop's mantle or bishop's collar.

To add the aventail and the bishop's collar to your coif, start at side X (Figure 15-1) on the right side. Extend your rows

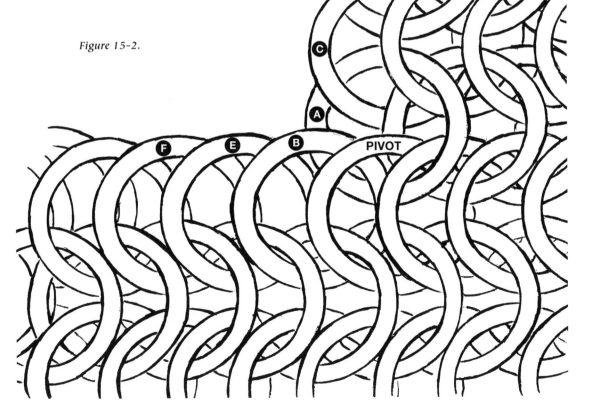

Figure 15-2.

Figure 15-3.

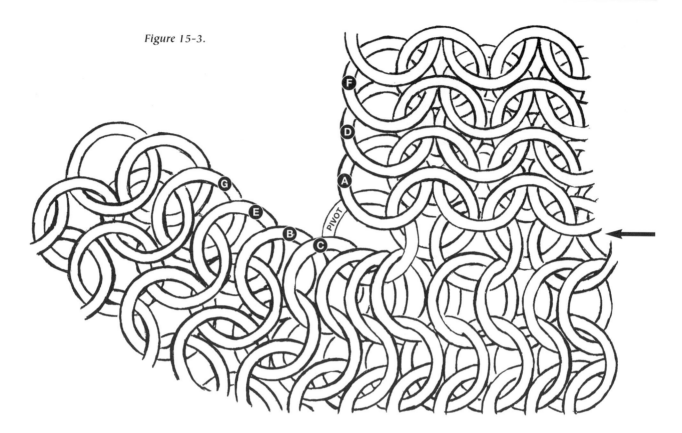

by 9 inches. You will be working a 9-inch piece of mail into flairs and adding it to the bottom of your coif as you go.

The directions to add a bishop's mantle to a coif are basically the same as those for making a bishop's mantle by itself (which follow shortly). In making a bishop's mantle by itself, you use a base of 6-on-2 mail around the neck. Starting at the point where the 4-on-1 pattern is added to the 6-on-2 pattern is the same as adding the mantle to the coif. This explains how to add the extra rings for the flairs.

On the diagram in Figure 15-1 at the beginning of this chapter, notice points G and F. Points G (there are two of them) are centered directly over the shoulders. Point F is the center of the back. The first point G should be about 2 inches from side X.

Figure 15-4.

Point F should be about 10 inches from side X. The final point G should be about 18 inches down from X.

The aventail is simply an extension of the rows you are adding to form mail that will cover the front of the neck. You will want to gradually round it into the face area under the chin. It is easier to do this if you first make an extension the length you desire to cover the front of the neck and then round it into the coif and add the little extension upward toward the top of the head so it can be fastened near the ear. Remember, there will be flairs in the middle of the aventail also.

For instructions on inserting these flairs, skip ahead a few pages to "Attention—Mantle Construction for Coifs." Your instructions will continue there.

If you want to be authentic in fastening this part up, leather ties can be used. However, these ties can be inconvenient. If you do use leather, use two ties: one at the end of the aventail and the other fastened into the mail by the ear. Then you can simply tie the two together when you put the coif on. You do not want to try to thread the leather through the links when you put it on: you cannot see what you are doing.

You can also fashion a hook on the end of the aventail and simply hook the aventail into the mail by the ear. There are also snaps, clips, or any number of other devices for fastening .

Figure 15-4 shows a close-up picture of actual mail formed into a square coif.

BISHOP'S MANTLE OR COLLAR

This is the basic design for a mantle with a 16-inch neck. It starts with a band of three rows of 6-on-2 mail, connected to the main mantle of 4-on-1 mail and ends with a three-row band of 6-on-2 mail. The top 6-on-2 rows should fit snugly around the neck, like a choker-type necklace. The bottom rows of 6-on-2 should lie just below the point of the shoulder. This design is very simple to alter for size, even after started, simply by adding more rows or columns.

Figures 15-5 and 15-6 depict mantles that I constructed, modeled by my son, David, and. my niece, Nikki. Mantles look good on anyone.

We start with the band of three rows of 6-on-2 mail. Connect two large rings, one small ring, two large rings, one small ring, etc., until you have a chain of 27 sets of large rings and 26 small rings.

Figure 15-5.

Figure 15-6.

Next, make two more chains of rings exactly the same as this one (Figure 15-7).

Take two of the chains and lay them side by side, slightly offset so that the large rings of one chain fit between the large rings of the other chain (Figure 15-8. You will attach these two chains together.

Take a small ring and attach the first set of large rings of chain one to the first set of large rings to chain two (Figure 15-9).

Next take a small ring and attach the first set of large rings of the first chain to the second set of large rings of the second chain, shown in Figure 15-10. Now you can easily see why they are offset and how they fit together.

Figure 15-11 shows the progression in linking the two chains. Continue by using a small ring to connect set two in the first chain to set two in the second chain. Then use a small ring to connect set

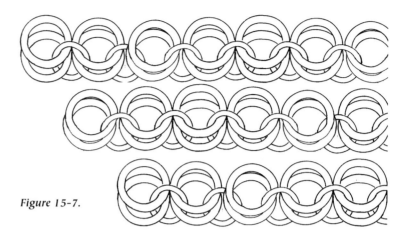

Figure 15-7.

Figure 15-8.

two of the first chain to set three of the second chain. Continue until you reach the end of the chain.Now you add the third chain to the first two, as shown in Figure 15-12. Simply start by using a small ring to attach the first set in the second chain to the first set in the third chain.

The next small ring will connect set two of the second chain to set one of the third chain. This is shown in Figure 15-13.

Continue in the same manner that you connected the first two chains together. Attach set two of the second chain to set two of the third chain and then set three of the second chain to set two of the third chain. Continue until this third chain is completely attached to the first two (Figure 15-14).

This in itself would make a nice necklace or bracelet. Of course, you could make this same design by using one long chain and doubling it back and forth to make three rows. But I find that a little more confusing and a lot more time consuming.

At this point you start adding the main section of 4-on-1 mail, which will consist of large rings. As usual take one open ring and add four closed rings to it and close the open ring, as in Figure 15-15.

Instead of working across the row, you will work down by columns. Figure 15-16 shows the next step. If this drawing confuses you, try turning it counterclockwise till the next side is up. Your next rings will be one open ring with two closed rings on it, and going up through the bottom ring in column 1 and the bottom ring in column 3.

Continue in this manner until you have 54 rings in column 1, as depicted in Figure 15-17.

Lay this piece next to your 6-on-2 strip, side by side, as in Figure 15-18. Use small links to connect the two strips. Use one to catch the first pair of large double links to the first two links in column 1.

Keep linking each set of double links in the 6-on-2 to the next two sets of rings in the 4-on-1

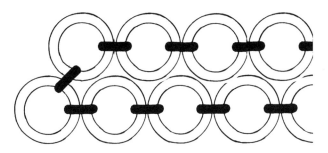

Figure 15-9.

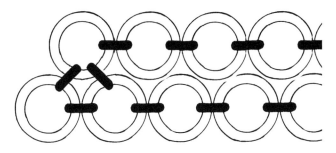

Figure 15-10.

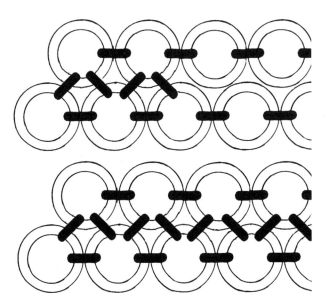

Figure 15-11.

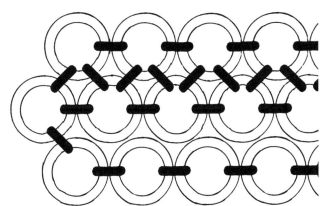

Figure 15-12.

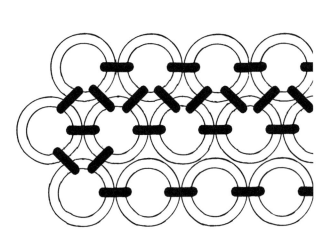

Figure 15-13.

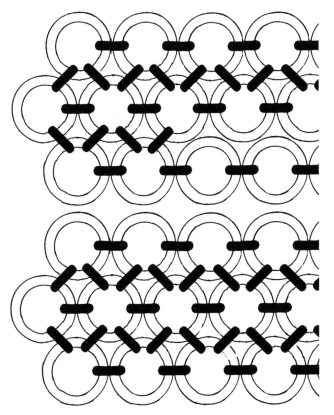

Figure 15-14.

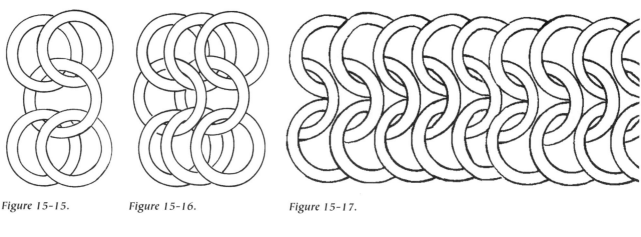

Figure 15-15.   Figure 15-16.   Figure 15-17.

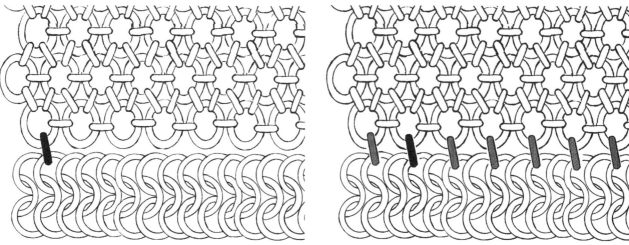

Figure 15-18.   Figure 15-19.

until you reach the end. Do not go through the same link in the 4-on-1 twice (Figure 15-19). This makes the transformation from 6-on-2 to 4-on-1.

ATTENTION—MANTLE CONSTRUCTION FOR COIFS

The next step will set up your flairs. This is where you start with when you add a bishop's mantle to a coif. Just to give you a break, here are some pictures of my son modeling a coif. The close-up picture is of the aventail.

Starting with column three of your 4-on-1 mail strip (or if you are adding this to a coif, on the last row of your mail), count down to between the fifth and sixth rings. Place an open ring there (Figure 15-23).

Next, count down seven more rings and place a second open ring between the seventh and eighth rings there. Continue this until you have added all seven extra rings for flairs. The last division between the last ring and the end should be between the sixth and seventh rings from that end. If you come across someone with a small neck and large shoulders you might wish to add these extra rings fifth or even every third ring instead of every seventh.

If you are adding to a coif, you will have a longer length and will have more than seven rings to add. Also, you will have to add a strip to go across the throat, as in Figure 15-1, for the aventail. To do that, add these rings to form the area across the throat. You will have to build the far side upward to form the I portion in Figure 15-1.

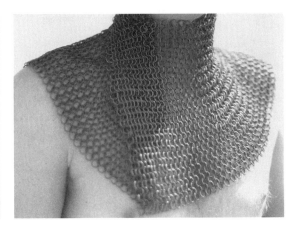

Figures 15-20, 15-21, and 15-22.

From this point, you can continue this in one of two ways. Either you simply add a normal set of columns and then go back and add the extra rings in the appropriate places, or you add the extra rings as you go along. To add them as you go along, add two closed rings instead of one when you come to those places (Figure 15-24).

Notice too in Figure 15-24 the rings labeled "a" and "b." These hold the extra rings you are adding and so have five rings going through them instead of the normal four. On the top side of each they connect to two rings, but on the bottom they go through three rings.

Where before the extra rings were between the sixth and seventh rings, the next column of rings will be between the seventh and eighth rings. Remember, you added a row. So the next set will be between the eighth and ninth rings and the next between the ninth and tenth, and so on.

Continue in this manner until you have reached the desired length. The measurement from the base of the neck to the point of the shoulder should be the same as between the beginning of the 4-on-1 mail and the last column you added.

To finish the mantle, you need only add three rows of 6-on-2 mail to form a matching edge for the top. It is done in the same way as the first three rows. Simply count the number of rings in your last column and divide by two. This is the number of the large sets of links you will need in your chains for the bottom trim.

Make three chains this length, put them

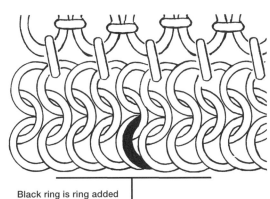

Black ring is ring added

Enlargement

Figure 15-23.

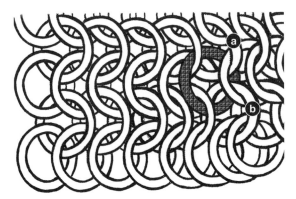

Figure 15-24.

together, and then attach them to the 4-on-1 mail
as you did before.

Leather lacing can be attached to the rings on
both sides of the mantle at regular intervals and used
to tie the mantle in place. Or, if you wish, you may
attach part of the collar together so that it has to be
placed on by putting it over the head and then using
hooks or catches to fasten the top near the neck.
Either way, your mantle is done.

Figure 15-25 shows Bill in his coif.

Figure 15-25.

Gauntlets

Gauntlets were first made like mittens—that is, with no individual fingers except for the thumb. The gauntlets also were not made separately, but rather attached to the sleeves, with a slit at the wrist area so they could be slipped off and left dangling when not in use. The misconception I find most often about gauntlets is that they were made totally of mail. Because it was, and still is, highly impractical for the palm portion to also be made of metal rings, it was made of leather. Palm mail would force the knight to hold his sword or lance with metal against metal, which does not make for a good grip—and a good grip might have meant the difference between living and dying.

The easiest and quickest way to make a usable gauntlet is to purchase heavy work gloves, pad the backs of them, and cover them in mail. This method is especially effective if you want individual fingers instead of a mitten-type gauntlet, but it can be used for a mitten style as well and will save hours and probably provide a more secure fit.

For those of you who prefer to work from scratch, I have provided full instructions. If you are using work gloves, you can still use the instructions for attaching the padding and mail.

In these instructions, I give you a pattern for mitten gauntlets made separately from the sleeves. You can adjust the length of the gauntlet to go as far up the arm as you wish; I recommend that you go at least 3 inches past the wrist.

Also note that the gauntlet flares out past the wrist. This is necessary not only because the arm is larger higher up, but also because you usually have a full-length sleeve of mail to go over. Keep this in mind when you are making measurements. I will discuss

gauntlets with individual fingers after this; the
basic construction techniques are the same.

To give you a general idea of the construction,
here's how the pieces fit together. First, there is
the palm area, made of leather. Then comes the
upper hand area. This consists of a leather base
next to the hand, on top of which is mounted
heavy padding. On top of the padding is the mail.
The top piece is larger because it will also cover
the side of the hand.

The first step is to trace your hand on a piece
of paper, just as you did in grade school. Allow a
little extra room at the tips of the fingers and
thumb for movement when you bend your hand
(Figure 16-1).

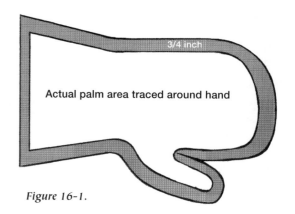

Figure 16-1.

Then you want to get together some fairly heavy leather for the palm area. The handiest
source of this is probably The Leather Factory, which carries all types of leather and has
very helpful employees. The piece you need is probably referred to as a "2- or 3-ounce
piece." Be sure that you get one pliable enough for the wearer's hand to move. While you are
at the store, also pick up a quantity of leather lacing. For a mitten-type gauntlet, you'll need
about 12 to 20 feet, depending on the type of stitch you use. Also pick up a leather needle for
the lacing.

WARNING: *Do not cut your leather until you are sure the measurement across the top edge of
the palm area (the part that will go across the wrist), doubled and plus 2 inches, is equal to the
circumference of the arm plus allowance for the seams. Check also at the wrist area and make sure
that you have room to get your hand into the gauntlet.*

The palm area is made in the following way. When you place your tracing on the leather,
make the cut a little larger than the tracing, about 3/4 inch all around. You can cut the leather
with a good pair of scissors (you do not need a special knife). Next, take a sharp knife and bevel
the edge of the leather all around. Bevel? All this means is gradually thinning the edge to not be
more than 1/16 inch wide to keep the edge from digging in and making a lump. There is a tool
made for this, but with a little care you can do it easily with a sharp knife. It doesn't have to be

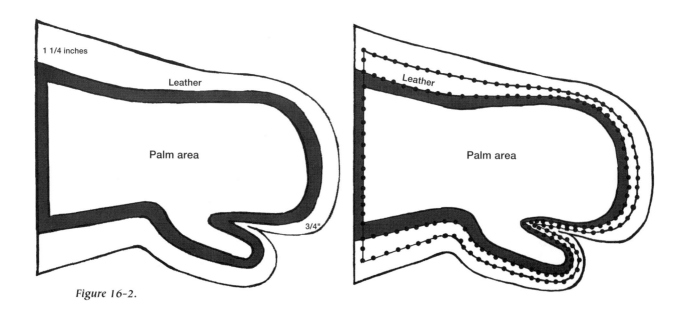

Figure 16-2.

perfect . . . no one is going to see it when you are done. Some people even skip this step. It depends on how exact you wish to be.

Next you make holes in the leather. For this I recommend that you use a leather punch. You can buy the inexpensive kind that you hit with a hammer or the handier but more expensive plier punch, depending on how much of this work you plan to do. Make your holes 1/4 inch apart and of a 1/8-inch diameter right on the outside of the line you traced of your hand. Instead of measuring all this, which would slowly drive you crazy, take a piece of mail, lay it on top of the leather where you want the holes, and mark in the center of each ring with a felt-tip pen. Be sure your mail is lying smoothly and evenly spaced. You need to make holes all around the outside, even across the wrist area.

The leather base for the top of the hand area is made in the same way but larger. Take a look at your hand. Notice that the fingers aren't as thick as the area at the wrist end. You can use your palm area that you just made to draw the pattern for this piece and then add 3/4 inch around the finger area, gradually increasing to 1 1/4 inches at the wrist area (refer to Figure 16-2).

Do not make the wrist area across any longer toward the elbow. The fingers should be about 1/2-inch thick and the wrist area approximately 1-inch thick. The additional 1/4 inch is for an overlap when lacing. If you are not making fighting mail, you can skip the leather here and just make a light padding to go under the mail so that it won't dig into your hand.

Next make your holes along the edges of this leather. The best way to do it is to place the palm piece on top and mark the holes through it. When you line them up, put the palm piece 1/4 inch farther in. In other words, while your holes in the palm-area leather are approximately 1/2 inch from the edge, the ones in your upper-hand leather will be 3/4 inch from the edge. You want the holes to line up exactly when you put the pieces together. I suggest that you start by marking the area at the fingers and thumb first.

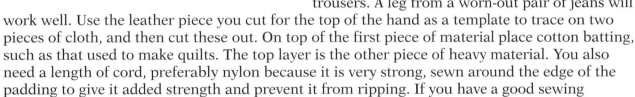

Figure 16-3.

Now you need to make the padding that will go between the mail and your hand. You need some heavy material, such as denim or twill or other fabric found in trousers. A leg from a worn-out pair of jeans will work well. Use the leather piece you cut for the top of the hand as a template to trace on two pieces of cloth, and then cut these out. On top of the first piece of material place cotton batting, such as that used to make quilts. The top layer is the other piece of heavy material. You also need a length of cord, preferably nylon because it is very strong, sewn around the edge of the padding to give it added strength and prevent it from ripping. If you have a good sewing machine, sew right over the cord. If not, sew along the side of it, on the inside. The padding when sewn will be a little smaller than the upper-hand leather.

As in Figure 16-3, take a marker and mark a line 1/2 inch in, all around the material. To allow the material to fold over without bunching, make cuts in the material at the tips of the fingers and around the end of the thumb, between the thumb and the hand and on the outside of the thumb near the hand. These cuts should only go in as far as the line

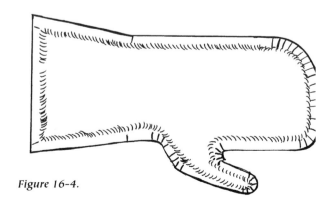

Figure 16-4.

where it will be folded over. As you read on, this becomes clearer.

As shown in Figure 16-4, place the cord on the material, just inside the line, starting at the top of the place where the gauntlet meets the arm. It is better to make the cord start and end here because it will not leave an uncomfortable lump on the edge of your hand. To make it a little easier, you may use a little glue or silicon to hold the cord in place

Now fold the cloth of the next section over the cord and sew it in place (Figure 16-5).

Figure 16-6 shows that the curved areas, such as the end of the mitten, are easier to sew if you make the cuts in the material at right angles, down to the sewing line. Just fold one flap at a time over the cord and sew it down. Each will slightly overlap the previous flap on the inside. The area at the base of the thumb and finger area will work the same way, but with the flaps leaving gaps on the inside.

As in Figure 16-7, once you have the cord sewn all around, overlap it across the top of the gauntlet and cut it off. Finish sewing across the top.

As shown in Figure 16-8, take padding (e.g., that used in quilting or available foam rubber or even layers of soft material) and cut to fit over the material. Next place the second piece of heavy material on top of this. Again, make cuts so that this can be sewn without bunching. Tuck the edge of the top piece of material under the padding and sew around the outside again. Then sew in a crisscross pattern (as in quilting) to hold the padding in place and keep it from sliding around.

At this point the gauntlet rather looks like an oven mitt, and it is basically the same as the top of one. You might even consider just using one or two such mitts for padding and save yourself a lot of sewing.

If you use a leather base, attach the padding to the leather. If you have an

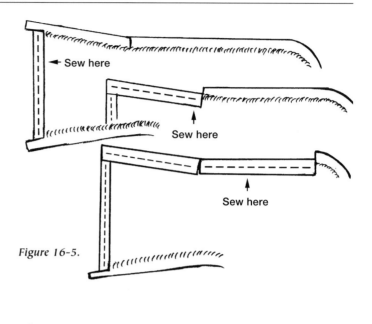

Figure 16-5.

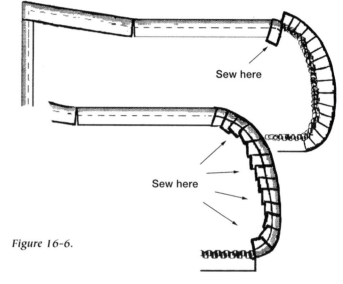

Figure 16-6.

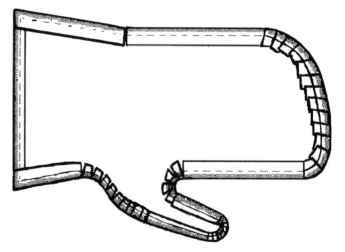

Figure 16-7.

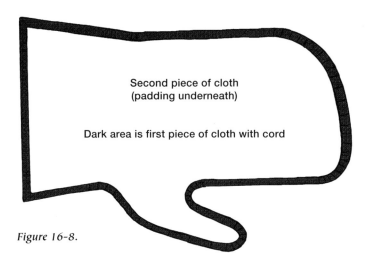

Second piece of cloth
(padding underneath)

Dark area is first piece of cloth with cord

Figure 16-8.

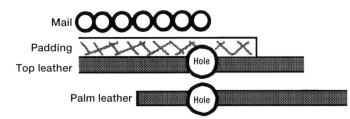

Mail

Padding

Top leather

Hole

Palm leather

Hole

Figure 16-9.

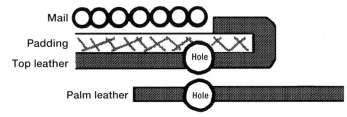

Mail

Padding

Top leather

Hole

Palm leather

Hole

Figure 16-10.

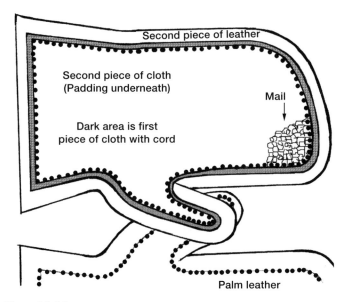

Second piece of leather

Second piece of cloth
(Padding underneath)

Mail

Dark area is first
piece of cloth with cord

Palm leather

Figure 16-11.

excellent machine, you can sew the padding on, but most machines won't handle a piece of material that thick and the leather, too. In this case, attach it with an adhesive; I recommend silicon rubber because it dries soft and flexible. You do not want something that dries rigid because you won't be able to bend your hand. Rub the silicon rubber into the leather and the cloth. Stick the two pieces together and let them dry for about an hour. Your cloth piece should fit just outside the holes in your leather but not all the way to the edge. There should be an extra 1/2 inch of leather all the way around. Next punch holes through the cloth to match the ones in the leather.

Figures 16-9 and 16-10 show how the two pieces (palm area and upper area) fit together. The cord sewn into the padding would be to the left of the hole in the upper layer. The leather of the top piece folds over the padding as shown in Figure 16-10.

Now you have the bottom and top of the glove. Next make the mail to cover the top. Simply make a piece and shape it around the form you have by using the same technique for doing points or rounding corners.

You have to stitch all these parts together. Don't worry; the instructions for stitching them are forthcoming. You cannot stitch them with just one piece of lacing, so I have included instructions for splicing in another piece of lacing.

Figure 16-11 shows you how to connect all the parts. Place the mail on top of the padding and leather. Starting at the wrist end, at the thumb side, lay the palm area next to it with the thumbs next to each other. They should be opposite, as in a mirror image. Slide the palm area under the top area until it reaches the edge of the holes but not past them. The palm area should now be under the edge of the top area: this is how the holes in the palm area pieces will be joined. However, for working purposes, just place them next to each other for now.

The following sequence takes you the rest of the way, figure by figure.

Figure 16-12: Take a piece of lacing, about 3 feet long, and attach it to a heavy darning needle or a leather needle. Go down through the second hole in the palm piece and up through the first hole, leaving about an inch of lacing through the hole. Next go down through the first ring in the mail and the first hole in the top piece and draw it tight to the first piece, while holding on to the end left sticking through the second hole. Be sure the link of mail you go through is firmly fastened and that the lacing will not slip between the join in the link. As you do this, the extra leather strip on the top piece will fold over the padding, effectively hiding any edge there. Figure 16-12 gives you a side view of this operation, and Figure 16-13 shows a top view of the same step.

It is extremely important that you check to make sure that the holes around the thumb area match perfectly *before you begin*. Although I have you starting at the top, wrist end, on the inside (thumb) side of the hand, you might first start at the tip of the thumb and work toward the first finger. This should ensure that you have the holes lined up properly.

Figure 16-14: Next go up through the second hole in the palm area (the same hole you went down through the first time) and down through the second ring of mail and the second hole in the top piece. Draw this tight, folding the leather strip over the padding.

Figure 16-15: This spiral stitch continues all the way around the edge of the gauntlet. After a few stitches, the end of the lacing you started with should be firmly fastened in place between the two layers.

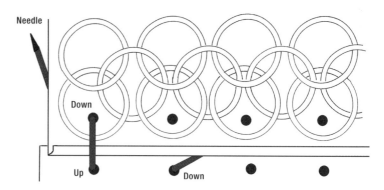

Figure 16-12.

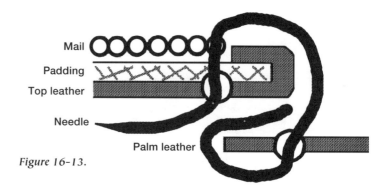

Figure 16-13.

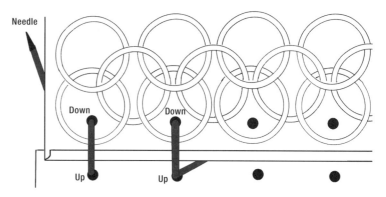

Figure 16-14.

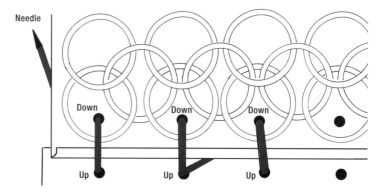

Figure 16-15.

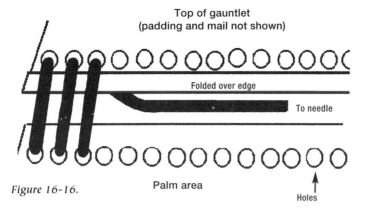

Figure 16-16.

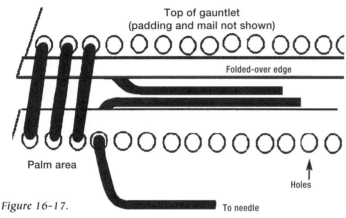

Figure 16-17.

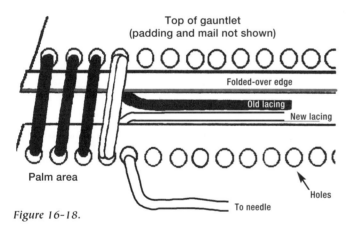

Figure 16-18.

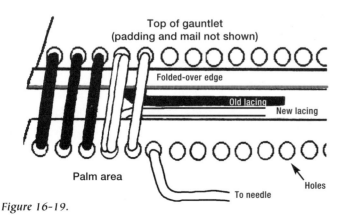

Figure 16-19.

You cannot easily handle a piece of lacing long enough to reach all around the glove, so you will use multiple shorter pieces. This means, however, that you will have to make a transition from the end of one piece of lacing to the beginning of the next lacing piece. No problem. Just leave an inch of lacing at the end of the old piece to be sandwiched between the layers, as when you started (Figure 16-16).

Figure 16-17: Start the second piece the same way you started originally. Lay its end alongside the end of the first piece of lacing. Go up through the next hole in the palm area.

Figure 16-18: Go down through your mail (not shown in diagram) and the top part of your gauntlet in the next hole. Keep your finger on the lacing end while you pull this tight. It will take a couple of loops before it is set in place. Go up through the next hole in the palm area.

Figure 16-19: From there, you go along as you have been lacing until you run out of lacing again.

When you reach the wrist area at the other side of the top of the glove, you can do a spiral stitch around the edges of the top piece, firmly attaching the mail and padding together. Continue around over the palm area section of the wrist until you come back to where you came up the side. Take your needle and slip it between the two pieces of leather going down the side for an inch or so, coming out on the inside of the glove. Cut the lacing close to the seam, and tuck the end in. One gauntlet down, one to go.

To make a gauntlet with individual fingers, you use the same method of construction. The differences are in cutting the original pattern, and allowing for seams between the fingers.

Figure 16-20: Start with the construction of the padding that fits under the mail. First, draw a pattern around your hand, with your fingers spread a little. Put the thumb out at almost a right angle to the hand.

Figure 16-21: Next, cut the hand piece apart, from the base of each finger to the wrist. Place this on the heavy cloth, spaced an inch apart. This will give you a seam of 1/2 inch on each side of the finger. When you cut down between the fingers, you also cut across in a T-shape at the base of the finger. Now you have material that can fold up around each finger.

Figures 16-22 and 16-23: You need to get rid of the extra material in the palm area, though. The easiest way to do this is to fold the extra material over and sew it down.

Next you place the cord around the edges, as you did in the mitten type. Remember that you want it to be slightly larger than the top of the finger, so that there is room to cover the sides of the finger and join with the palm portion.

Again, when you cut the leather for the palm area and the upper area, make sure that these pieces are larger than for the finger. Also, keep in mind the thickness of the hand, both in the finger area and in the palm area, when cutting.

Check out the half-gauntlets in Chapter 18.

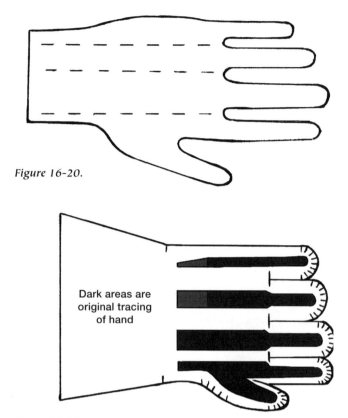

Figure 16-20.

Figure 16-21.

Dark areas are original tracing of hand

Fold here

Fold here

Figure 16-22.

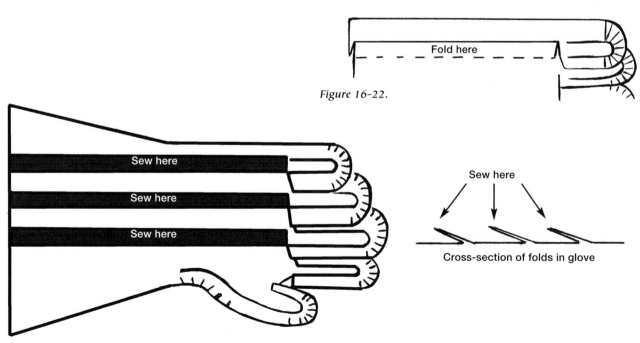

Figure 16-23.

Sew here

Sew here

Sew here

Sew here

Cross-section of folds in glove

CHAPTER 17

Care and Polishing of Mail

The best way to care for mail is to be careful not to get it wet. Moisture is the worst enemy of any metal. It will make your steel rust, your copper turn black, and your brass corrode.

Naturally, such care is not always possible. If you are outside at a festival you can get rained on, have a beverage spilled down your front, or end up very sweaty, all of which may cause your mail to be tarnished. In fact, just normal moisture in the air eventually causes tarnishing.

If you use electric-fence wire, which is galvanized steel, you won't have much of a problem with rust, unless it is exposed to water for long periods.

Dealing with excessive moisture, such as rain, is just a matter of drying it off as soon as possible. If you are not going to use the mail for a long period, store it in an airtight package. Put in some of those little packages of desiccant (e.g., silica) that prevent moisture, wrap the whole thing in plastic, and tape it up well.

Sooner or later, though, you will have to clean it. For steel, or galvanized steel, the biggest problem is rust. With any of the commercial rust removers,, just follow the directions. Although it is expensive, I recommend Naval Jelly, which works quickly and easily. Be sure to wear protective gloves, however, because it is very corrosive.

Once the rust has been removed, you can coat your mail with spray lacquer or varnish—but not too thickly. And spray it from both sides of the mail. This will help keep rust from coming back. Just remember that varnish does become darkened and discolored over time. To remove it, use paint remover and wash it very well; then you dry the mail completely and recoat. Plastic-type clear varnish works a little better than others and does not get discolored as quickly. Varathane is a very good brand of varnish.

Waxing is another way to protect your mail. Various brands of car and floor wax work fine. And the mail can be buffed with an attachment on an electric drill.

Here is an interesting old formula for cleaning that I came across. Once you have completely cleaned your mail, wash it again with ammonia, and rinse it well. Place the mail in an oven and heat to dry it thoroughly. Next oil it well with sweet oil. Then place it in a heavy bag and pour in quicklime—but be careful: quicklime can cause severe burns. Shake it to make sure that the lime completely coats the mail. Leave it in the bag for two days. Remove the mail, wearing gloves to protect your hands, and use a stiff brush to clean the quicklime off the mail. Then take a softer brush or a buffer on a drill and polish the mail. This is supposed to keep rust from forming for a long, long time.

To clean copper links used as accents or in inlaid designs there are many commercial cleaners. Many of them work well, but I don't use them. I am basically a very lazy person, which means I hate to scrub things. So I use catsup to clean copper. Don't believe it? Try it on an old penny. Just take straight catsup, any brand right out of the bottle, and pour some on a penny. In just a second you can see the change. Of course, it does help if you take your finger and smear it around a little, but this doesn't require any great effort. To clean mail, use a soft brush to get in between the links. One word of warning, however: don't let the catsup dry! It gets very crusty and is a pain to clean off. After cleaning, coat your mail with varnish or wax to prevent future discoloration.

Brass is a beautiful metal to use in mail. Even though it is expensive, it gives an almost gold-like look when it is clean. Dirty brass does not look so attractive, however. Cleaning brass usually requires a great deal of scrubbing and polishing, and it becomes tarnished rapidly.

Again, there are many commercial cleaners available; Brasso is one of the better known ones. Most require that you apply the cleaner, wait for it to dry, and then buff it off, which is difficult with mail. Getting in between the links to buff even with an electric drill or Dremel tool is time consuming. Because I am lazy, I looked for an easier method. This one you will really have trouble believing, so get some brass and try it out. It works great.

Buy some cheap metal cleaner. If you have a dollar store in your town, look for MWW All-Purpose Brass, Chrome, & Metal Polish, which costs $1 for a 16-ounce jar (or there may be other similar products available). In the same store you will probably find a dollar bottle of Worcestershire sauce. Pick that up, too.

Take a small dish and pour out a blob of metal cleaner and then add the same amount of Worcestershire sauce. Mix well. Take a clean rag, dip it into the mixture and apply it to your brass. If you hit a particularly tarnished place, use a little more Worcestershire sauce. You don't have to leave this on very long. Rinse it off; dry your mail, and coat it.

I do not recommend using straight Worcestershire sauce because it may result in brass that looks as if it has become crystallized. Also, this may occur if you leave the mixture of metal polish and Worcestershire sauce on too long. If this happens, don't panic. Simply mix up a fresh batch of cleaner and apply again. It may take a little rubbing, but the crystal look will be removed. Be sure to wash and dry the mail thoroughly.

Speaking of cleaning metal, I will add this one for silver. Not much silver is used in the construction of mail, but you may have a cup or tray around that needs cleaning. Take a container big enough to completely immerse the object to be cleaned and fill it with a strong solution of salt water. Next tear up some pieces of aluminum foil and toss them into the container. Don't be stingy with the foil, which leeches off the tarnish on the silver and absorb it. Put your silver item in the pot and set it to one side for a day. When you take the silver out, wash it well in soapy water; it should become bright and shiny. If the silver is badly tarnished you may have to break down and use the conventional cleaners or polish it with toothpaste.

I wish you happy polishing. I hope you have enjoyed learning to construct mail and by now have a complete outfit. May it last you many years. Also, if shared with the right people these tips on cleaning metals, especially the copper and brass ones, might even earn you a free dinner. (Many housewives really hate to scrub that stuff.) Enjoy.

At some point you will probably have a link break. Replacing it should be no real problem. Simply study the pattern around the link to see where it connects. Checking for loose or broken links regularly is a good idea. It is easier to fix a small problem than to fix a big problem that got out of hand.

CHAPTER 18

Jewelry

This chapter deals with ideas and designs for jewelry. I start with a headpiece because it is one of the first items that people ask me about. From there I cover bracelets and necklaces, handflowers, half-gauntlets, and then a design of my own I call a shoulder necklace. From these ideas you should be able to design many more pieces of jewelry or overblouses or skirts.

Most of these designs are done in 6-on-2 mail. I find this more versatile for jewelry because it is easier to achieve a lacy effect with it. Some pieces use both the 6-on-2 and the 4-on-1 patterns. Be sure you are familiar with joining the two types together.

TRIANGULAR HEADPIECE

Headpieces are simply decorative caps for women. This particular design is a series of triangles made from 6-on-2 mail and connected by chains. In the diagrams you will notice that the connecting chains are depicted as wandering around, instead of lying straight. The reason is that the cap does not lie flat but is curved, which conforms to the top of the head.

We start by constructing the basic triangles needed. Figure 18-1 shows one triangle. Begin by making a chain

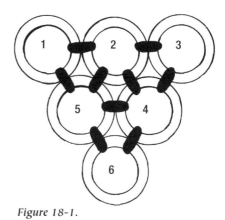

Figure 18-1.

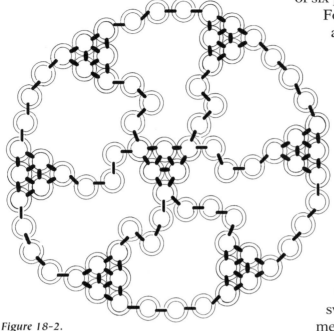

Figure 18-2.

of six pairs of large rings, joined by five small rings. Fold the fourth ring back between the second and third and join it there with a small ring. Now take a small ring and join between the second and fifth rings. Next a small ring will join the first and fifth rings. The last small ring joins the sixth and fourth rings.

Now that you have made one of these, make 12 more, for a total of 13 triangles. I find it faster and much less confusing to make the individual parts and then assemble them.

Using this technique is helpful when you are making up your own designs. Make the basic shapes you wish to incorporate and then use tie wire to see whether they fit together properly and hang correctly. The tie wire is easy to bend and can be quickly switched from one ring to another for adjustments. When you find the correct placement you can than replace it with a more solid ring.

Make 22 small chains of three sets of large links joined by two small links. These will be used to join the triangles to form the cap.

Take seven of the triangles and form them into the crown of the cap using 12 of the small chains, as shown in Figure 18-2.

Next, place the triangle that fits over the forehead. Use two more of the small chains to attach it, as in Figure 18-3.

The next step begins to build the sides and back. Take two more small chains and attach a triangle as shown in Figure 18-4.

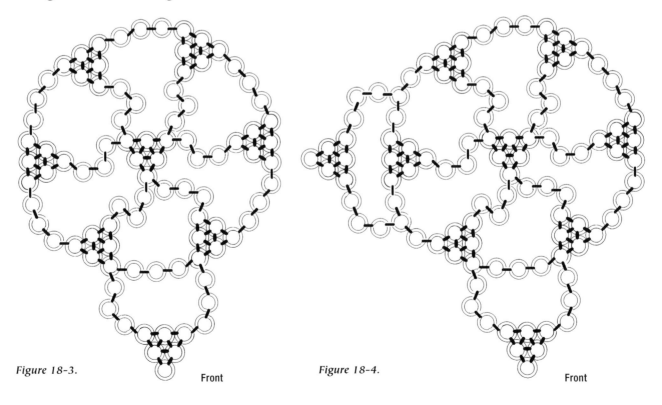

Figure 18-3.   Front

Figure 18-4.   Front

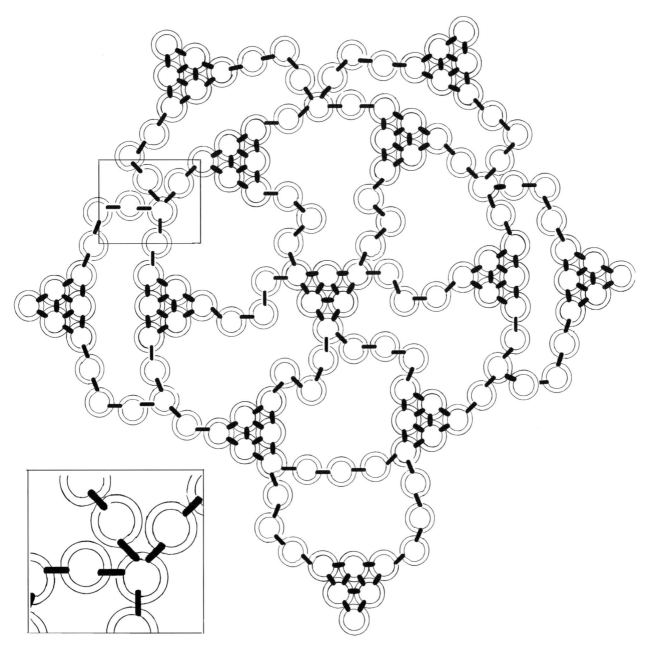

Figure 18-5.
Inset.

Figure 18-5 shows three more sections added to form the back and the other side. Use four more of the small chains to attach these two additional triangles.

Notice the inset in Figure 18-5 showing a close-up of the area where one section that was added meets the other section you are adding.

The end links of the three links in the small chains are both attached to the same link in the cap. However, the end links are not attached to each other because the way the headpiece drapes pulls these links away from each other.

Now you have to lengthen the back portion. Take two of the small chains and attach one more triangle at the very back of the headpiece, as shown in Figure 18-6.

After this piece is added you need to add the same type of piece on each side, as shown in Figure 18-7.

Figure 18-6.   *Figure 18-7.*

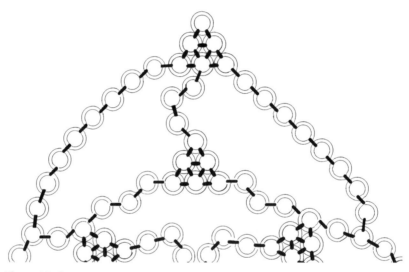

Figure 18-8.

Figure 18-9.   *Figure 18-10.*   *Figure 18-11.*

The last step is to add the final long piece to the back. Make two chains of eight sets of double-large links, joined by seven small links. Then make a chain of four sets of double-large links joined by three small links. Attach them to the last triangle and the back of the headpiece, as shown in Figure 18-8.

Notice that the chains of eight sets do not join directly to the point of the triangles in the headpiece, but in the middle of the chain of three connecting them. The chain of four sets joins the bottom point of the middle triangle in the headpiece to the middle ring of the top of the triangle you are adding.

Your headpiece is complete now. To show you how it looks on an actual head, see Figures 18-9 through 18-11, showing Nikki wearing one.

FLOWER HEADPIECE

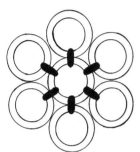

Figure 18-12.

Another design for making a headpiece is to use the flowerlike design of the 6-on 2 mail, as shown in Figure 18-12, and connect it together by chains of 6-on-2.

Since I have given detailed instructions for the triangular headpiece, I don't think you need great detail for this one because it is made in a very similar manner. I have provided a good diagram to guide you.

Figure 18-13 shows the overall design for this headpiece. To begin with, you make 10 of the flower sets, 8 chains of sets of 4 large double rings connected with 3 small rings, and 10 chains of sets of 8 sets of large double rings connected by 7 small rings. Then simply connect them together as shown in the diagram.

Of course both of these headpieces can be added to make them longer in the back and sides. You can use larger triangles or flowers, or you can start with a solid cap of 6-on-2 or 4-on-1 mail, as in the rounded coif, and then add these designs to the cap for a lacy effect on the sides and back. The variations are limited only by your imagination.

Figure 18-14 shows headpieces modeled by Nikki and Christine Fedele.

BRACELETS AND ARMBANDS

Bracelets are one of the easiest and quickest pieces of mail to make. An armband is simply an extended bracelet in that it is just a little longer and generally wider. Therefore, I mention armbands only in passing since any of the bracelet designs can be used for them.

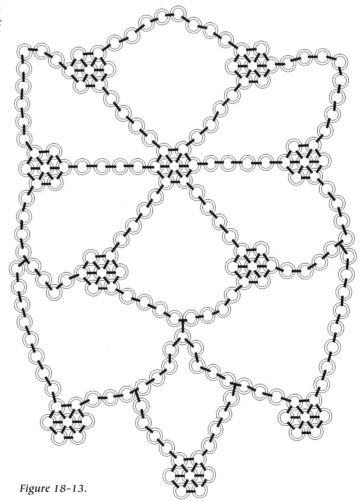

Figure 18-13.

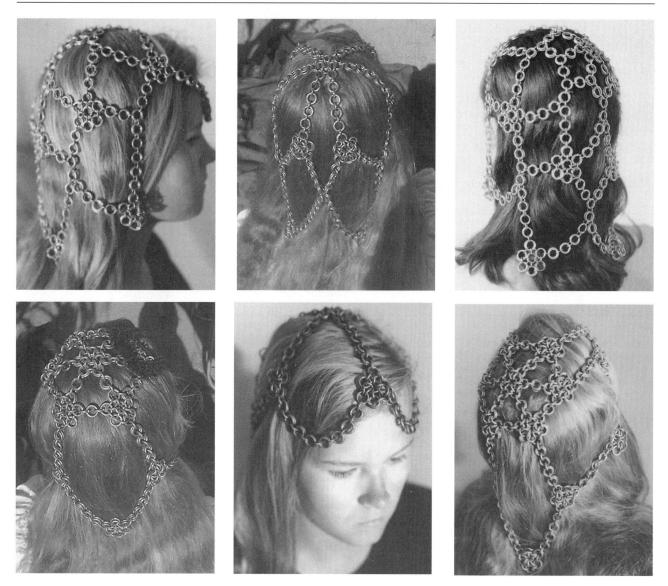

Figure 18-14.

The simplest bracelet is a strip of 4-on-1 mail, as shown in Figure 18-15. If you don't know how to make this, refer to the "Bishop's Mantle" section toward the end of Chapter 15.

Figure 18-16 shows a bracelet constructed as illustrated in Figure 18-15, except that the middle column of rings is smaller. Changing the size of the rings or the gauge of the wire or combining different ones can produce a totally different look. This technique also makes the bracelet stiffer, with the rings holding their shape better.

The next simplest bracelet (Figure 18-17) makes it two or more columns wider.

Another simple bracelet is a band of 6-on-2 mail, as shown in Figure 18-18. This design can also be made wider or can be made with individual "flowers" that are then connected at one point or two points. (See Chapter 12 for edging design ideas and the "Bishop's Mantle or Collar" section of Chapter 15 for construction techniques.)

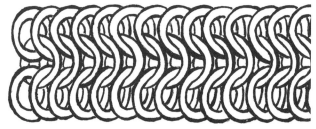

Figure 18-15

Figure 18-16.

Figure 18-17.

Figures 18-19a and 18-19b show two views of bracelets made from the 6-on-2 mail described above.

From here the next natural step is a combination of the two types of mail. Figures 18-20 and 18-21 give you the general idea. If you need directions for combining the two, they are covered in Chapter 11 in the "Joining 4-on-1 and 6-on-2 Mail" section and again in Chapter 15 in the "Bishop's Mantle and Collar" section.

Figures 18-22, 18-23, and 18-24 provide some additional ideas for combing the two mails. As you can see, with just a little change the whole look of the piece can be a big change. For instance, try eliminating the 4-on-1 mail in one of the designs and just using the 6-on-2. You still get the flower, triangle, or diamond area in the middle, and it is not quite so wide. With a little thought and imagination, the variations are endless.

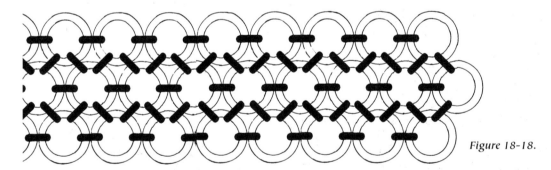

Figure 18-18.

Figure 18-19a.

Figure 18-19b.

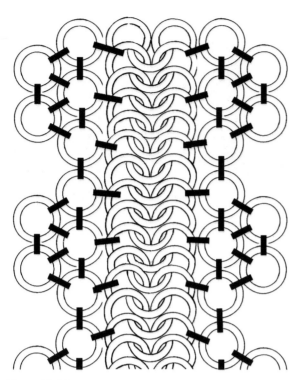

Figure 18-20.

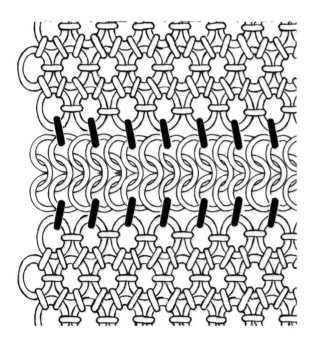

Figure 18-21.

Figure 18-22.

Figure 18-23.

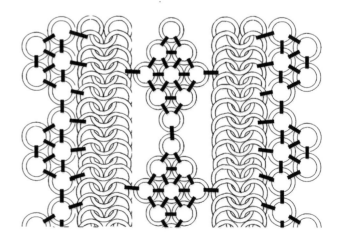

Figure 18-24.

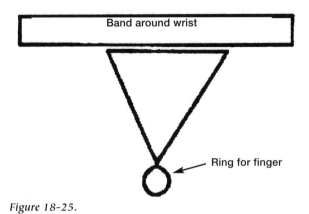

Band around wrist

Ring for finger

Figure 18-25.

HANDFLOWERS

Handflower is a common name for a bracelet that continues over the back of the hand and loops around the middle finger, as shown in the Figure 18-25 diagram.

The bracelet portion can be made in any of the designs described above. The triangular piece that goes over the back of the hand can be anything from 4-on-1 mail brought to a point to strips of 6-on-2 mail in chains just on the edge of the hand.

Instead of dealing with many diagrams, I include a few different pictures of handflowers in Figure 18-26. The designs are obvious enough to give you the details to make them.

Remember that you can also completely fill in the triangular area on the back of the hand. For example, you might inlay a small cross. Use your imagination; the possibilities are endless. (Refer to Chapter 20 for additional photographs of handflowers.)

Figure 18-26.

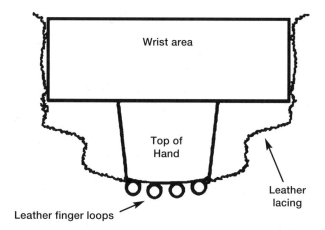

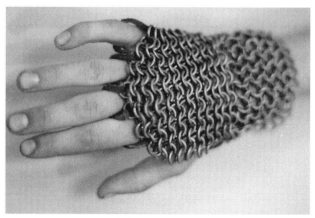

Figure 18-27.

HALF-GAUNTLETS

What I call a *half-gauntlet* is the male version of a handflower (Figure 18-27). Men seem to prefer heavier looking mail, so I usually use a solid band of 4-on-1 or 6-on-2 for the wrist area and continue it to cover the back of the hand—even though any of the basic bracelet designs will work for these. Then I use leather lacing through the mail itself to form the finger loops and across the palm and lacing up the wrist.

Again, instead of numerous diagrams, I am including two detailed pictures of some half-gauntlets.

Figure 18-28.

NECKLACES

Many of the simpler designs for the bracelets can also be made for necklaces. The three strands of 6-on-2 mail make a very beautiful choker. I use this for the basic layout of many necklaces, adding either triangles or flowers in the front to make different designs.

Most of the information for making these necklaces is contained in the previous section on bracelets or in the chapters referred to in that section. I will not repeat it here. Instead, take a look at some of the different necklaces I have mad. (Figure 18-29). You shouldn't have any problem figuring them out. Modeling the necklaces are Nikki and Christine Fedele.

For even more ideas, check out the next section on shoulder necklaces. These can also be made as short necklaces. And be sure to check out the photo gallery in Chapter 20, where. I have included more necklaces.

SHOULDER NECKLACES

I must make a personal comment here. I am not a person who cheerfully walks into a shop and, without batting an eye, spends several hundreds of dollars on jewelry . . . or anything else. When forced to do so, I usually cry. So when I wanted some mail I found myself making my own—and it was much cheaper.

I not only have this aversion to spending money, but am also lazy, as I have mentioned several other places in this book. This caused me to wonder: why use a piece of mail jewelry as

Figure 18-29.

only a necklace? Surely, it could be used as a belt also. From there the idea expanded, and the shoulder necklace was invented.

This one piece can function as a large necklace and a belt, and can also be divided into two pieces and worn as a belt with a matching necklace. There is also the possibility of a necklace and a matching headpiece. Such a versatile piece is not only handy to have but easy to sell as well.

The shoulder necklace is designed with the front and back pieces in the same pattern. Thus when worn around the shoulders or as a full belt, the front and back look the same. When the two pieces are separated, only the middle portion of the back is removed. Thus the back portion is divided at a point that makes it a bit smaller than the front portion. This back portion makes the matching necklace, while the larger piece makes the matching belt. The last necklace in this section, the solid triangle, is shown as two pieces that detach evenly, but this can be changed to two uneven pieces if you wish.

The following are directions for making three slightly different shoulder necklaces, with but the first one being smaller. All are made strictly with the 6-on-2 pattern, but this doesn't mean that you couldn't incorporate 4-on-1 into a design of your own.

Small Triangle

For the small-triangle shoulder necklace you need 22 of the triangle-shaped pieces depicted in Figure 18-30. This is 6-on-2 mail, so there are two large rings to each set connected by a small ring (the small rings shown in black).

As in the previous section on headpieces, I find it easier and less confusing to make the components of the piece and then assemble them. I also strongly suggest that you make diagrams of your completed designs. Don't rely on memory.

Next you will take six of the triangles and fit them together as in Figure 18-31. This design makes a nice necklace with the simple addition of some chains on each side.

Now take six more triangles and make another one just like the first.

Next, you make the shoulder area. This part will drape over the shoulder when worn as a full necklace.

First make three chains of three sets of large double rings connected by two small rings.

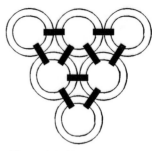

Figure 18-30.

Take three triangles and connect them as shown in Figure 18-32. Again, with chains added to the corners, this makes a very nice necklace. You need two of these pieces, so make another one just like the first.

The last pieces are the ones that will join the four pieces you have now made. So you need to make four of them.

First make four chains of three sets of double rings connected by two small rings.

Take one triangle and fasten one chain to it. The other end of this chain is fastened to the triangle in the shoulder piece. On the opposite corner of the new triangle that you have added, fasten one set of double rings with one small ring, as in Figure 18-33.

Figure 18-31.

On the opposite side of the shoulder section, attach one of the chains of three double links. To this attach another triangle. Then attach a single set of double links to the other side of the triangle you have just added. At this point you should have completed the design in Figure 18-33. This makes an even nicer necklace.

Now attach the shoulder piece to the front portion, as in Figure 18-34. Attach the other shoulder piece to the other side of this same front piece.

The last step is to take two jewelry clips and attach the back in the same manner. Leather thongs can also be used. The reason the back is attached with clips

Figure 18-32.

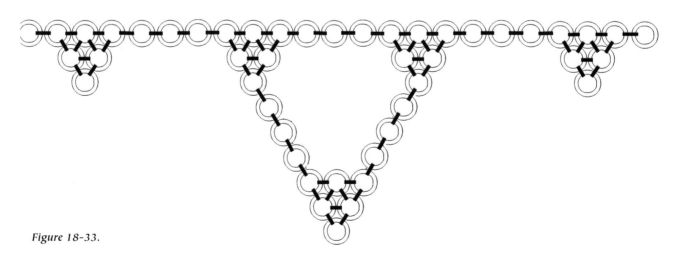

Figure 18-33.

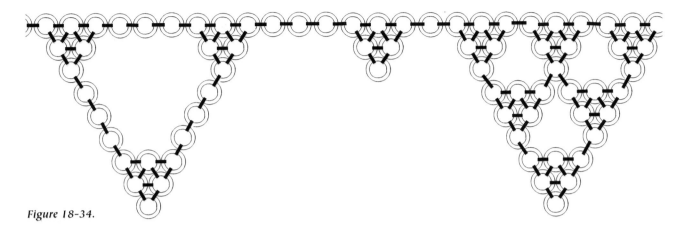

Figure 18-34.

Figure 18-35.

Figure 18-36.

is so that it can be detached from the front.

When the whole is attached and placed over the head it makes a necklace that drapes over the shoulders. Figure 18-35 shows how it looks on Nikki.

When one side is unfastened, the piece can be placed around the waist to form a belt, as shown in Figure 18-36.

When the back portion is unfastened on both sides, the back can be fastened with another chain or a leather thong to form a short necklace, and the front can be used as a matching belt in the same manner.

The ends of the front piece can also be clipped to the middle portion of the front and used as a headpiece, with the back used as a matching necklace.

Large Triangle

This shoulder necklace is similar to the small triangle, but it is larger and drapes farther over the shoulders. It is the most popular one I make.

Start with the triangular shape shown in Figure 18-37; you'll need 20 of these triangles. Notice that they have four sets of large double rings across each side instead of three sets as in the last necklace.

As in the previous necklace, take six of the triangles and form them into one large triangle, as in Figure 18-38. Take six more and make another large triangle. You need two of them.

The next step is to form the shoulder areas: you will need to make two of these pieces. Start by making the following:

- Six chains of eight sets of large double links connected by seven small links

- Two chains of seven sets of large double links connected by six small links
- Two chains of five sets of large double links connected by four small links.

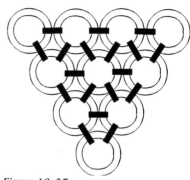

Figure 18-37.

Refer to Figure 18-39 to see how they are placed together. Notice that on the bottom of the point, one set of links is seven sets and the other is eight sets. The set of seven will be the front of the shoulder, while the set of eight will be to the back. This allows the necklace to drape at the middle of the arm, which is closer to the front of the body than to the back of the body.

All that's left is to join the two pieces, as shown in Figure 18-40. Be careful that the lower set of seven double rings is next to the front piece. Notice that the join is not made at the triangle of the back piece, but at the first link in the chain of eight sets. At the other end of the back section, a jewelry clip or leather thong is tied to the last ring of the set of eight, again not in the triangle.

Now attach the other shoulder piece to the other side of the front, being careful to place the lower set of seven next to the front.

If you compare the differences between these first two shoulder necklaces, you can see that it takes very little change in design to make a big change in looks.

Figure 18-41 shows this shoulder necklace worn in several ways by Nikki and Christine. Notice the different look created when the belt is worn with the main triangles to the front or to the side. Be sure to check the photos in Chapter 20.

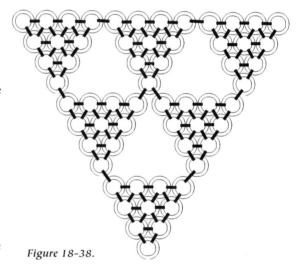

Solid Triangle

This last necklace is another variation on the triangle. With this design, however, you start by making the belt portion first. Make two chains of 33 sets of large double rings connected by 32 small rings.

Next make 10 chains of eight sets of large double rings connected by seven small rings. Attach these chains to the long chain you first made, as in the diagram in Figure 18-42. Five small chains will be attached to each long chain. Remember you are making two sides, each exactly alike, front and back.

Now add some triangles. You will need four triangles that have four sets of large double rings on each side. You will also need two large triangles that have seven

Figure 18-38.

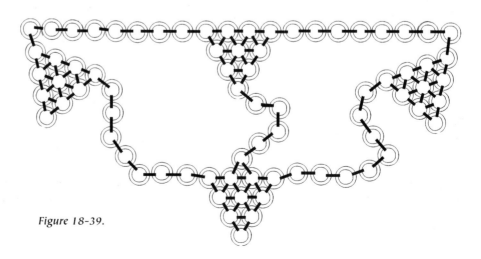

Figure 18-39.

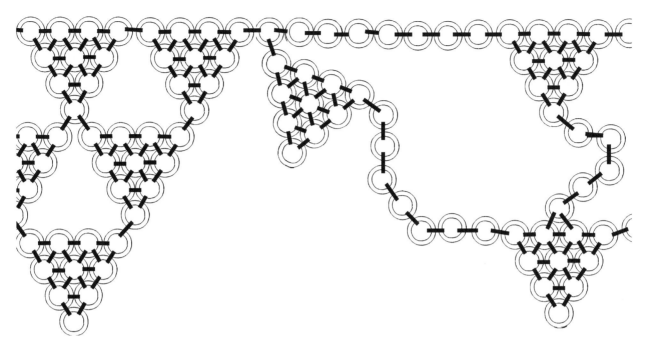

Figure 18-40.

Figure 18-41.

sets of large double rings on each side.

Figure 18-43 shows how the triangles are attached. One large triangle is placed in the middle with a small triangle on each side.

Figure 18-42.

Notice that the small and large triangles are joined by two large double links, and the second point from the belt is connected to the first of these links, not the end of the triangle.

Now that you have completed one side, make the other side exactly the same.

Attach leather thongs or jewelry clips to the end links. Your shoulder necklace is finished. It can be worn in the various ways that the other shoulder necklaces are worn.

A slight variation on this is to make the first loop from the long chain six large double links instead of eight and attach the

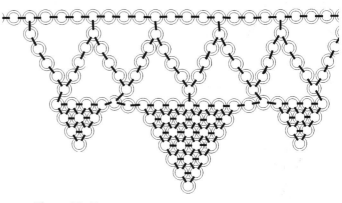

Figure 18-43.

small triangle to the fifth set, leaving only one set between that one and the link attached to the belt at the second point. This makes the design angle more into a curve

Nikki models this type of shoulder necklace in Figure 18-44.

• • •

I hope you have fun with these shoulder necklaces and come up with many new and different versions. Remember, with imagination, you can design stunning original versions that are all your own.

Figure 18-44.

CHAPTER 19

Additional Types of Mail

To round out this book, I include a quick description of several other types of mail. Let's go back to the beginning for a minute. Remember that there was 4-on-1 mail, then 6-on-1 mail. I also mentioned that you could make 8-on-1 or even 10-on-1 mail in the same manner.

The point I am making here is that the 6-on-2 pattern can be varied in the same way. For instance you can make an 8-on-2, 9-on-2, or 12-on-2 mail.

In the case of the 6-on-2 mail the rows are offset diagonally to allow for connecting. This is because you have six small rings in three sets of two links each to connect in three directions. Therefore, the large links must be offset to form a triangular pattern of large links (three sides to connect together).

In the case of the 8-on-2 mail the rows are kept at direct right angles to each other. They line up directly even with each other to form a square design. This is simply because if there are eight small links, there are four sets of two links each to connect in four directions. Therefore, they must connect at right angles, or in straight columns forming a square design (four sides to connect together). I do not include a detailed explanation of how to do this type of pattern. Besides my thinking that I think you are experienced enough by now to figure it out yourself, it is just like the 12-on-2 square design, which I do give you instructions for. Just use groups of eight small rings, instead of twelve.

In the case of the 9-on-2 mail the rows are at a diagonal, as in the 6-on-2 mail, and form a triangular design. This is simply because if you have nine small links, you have three sets of three links each to connect in three directions. Therefore, they connect to form a triangle (three sides to connect together). I am not including a detailed explanation of how to do this type either. It is just like the 12-on-2 triangular design, which I do give instructions for. Just use groups of nine small rings instead of twelve.

In the case of 12-on-2 mail it is a little different. The 12 small rings can be divided in two ways. First, you may have four sets of three links each. Second, you may have six sets of two each. So although both are 12-on-2 mail, they are totally different. The first is a square design, and the second is a triangular design as in the 6-on-2 mail.

Beyond 12-on-2 is really impractical to make mail in these patterns. A 16-on-2 would have four sets of four links going in four directions to make a square-type mail. However, if you try making the square type of 12-on-2 you will discover that three rings are hard enough to handle.

12-ON-2 MAIL SQUARE DESIGN

When working with so many small rings in a design, it is more practical to use them as the closed rings instead of the open rings. You will use the large rings as the connecting (open) rings. Also, you will work from the inside out, so to speak. You are going to make the center of the mail first, with connections in all directions. Then when the piece reaches the size you wish, you can add the outside row of large rings.

Figure 19-1

First take one large open ring and place on it 12 small closed rings. Close your ring. Next take another large open ring and place it exactly the same way on top of the other large ring. You'll end up with 12 small rings on two large rings (Figure 19-1).

Next take nine small closed rings on one large open ring and go through three of the small rings in your first set (9 + 3 = 12). Keep in mind that you are doing a design that has four sets of three rings going in four different directions (Figure 19-2).

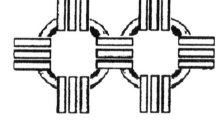

Figure 19-2

Now, again take a large open ring and insert it exactly the same way on top of the last large ring, so that you have two large rings on top of each other.

Add another set of rings in exactly the same way. Be sure that you choose the three small rings that are in the middle of the last set. In other words, you should have three small rings at the top of the large rings, three small rings at the bottom of the large rings, and three small rings attached to the large rings on each side (Figure 19-3).

The beginning of the next row will start with nine small rings on one large ring and attached to the three small rings at the bottom of the first row. Again, place your second large

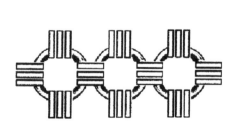

Figure 19-3

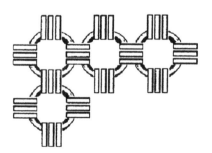

Figure 19-4

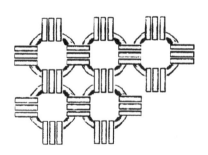

Figure 19-5

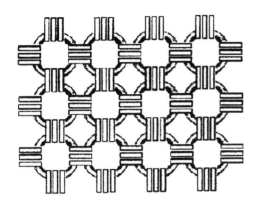

Figure 19-6

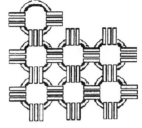

Figure 19-7

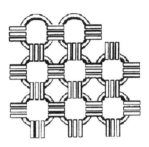

Figure 19-8

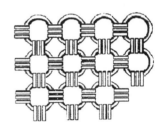

Figure 19-9

ring on top of the first one (Figure 19-4).

The second set of rings in your second row will have only six small rings added to the large ring. Then go through three small rings of the first set of the second row and three small rings of the bottom of the second set of rings of the first row (3 + 3 + 6 = 12) (Figure 19-5).

Keep adding rings in the same manner until you reach the size you want. Figure 19-6 shows more rings added.

That pretty well covers how to do it. You can add large rings to the outside rows easily. Start in a corner and use a large ring with only six small rings on it and go through the three small rings of the edge piece (Figure 19-7).

The next set of large rings will only use three small rings and picks up three rings from the first edge piece and three from the next inside piece (Figure 19-8).

Figure 19-9 shows going around the corner. Just continue in the same manner until you reach where you started. It is very simple.

12-ON-2 MAIL TRIANGULAR DESIGN

Again, when working with so many small rings it is easier to make them the closed rings and use the large rings as open rings.

Start by taking one large ring and threading on 12 small closed rings. Close the ring. Then take another large ring and thread it through right next to the first large ring. Close that ring. You now have 12 small rings on 2 large rings.

The next step is to take a large open ring and thread on 10 small closed rings. Thread the large open ring through two of the small rings on the first set you did. Close your ring. Then take another large open ring and thread it through exactly as you did the last large ring. Close this ring (refer to Figure 19-10).

At this point you have a chain of 10 small rings: 2 large rings—2 small rings—2 large rings—10 small rings.

Figure 19-10.

The next large ring has 10 small rings added to it and will be threaded through the middle 2 small rings of the end of the chain you are making. Again, you add another large ring exactly on top of this one (Figure 19-11).

As you can see, this allows you the four extra small rings on both the top and bottom of your chain to add your large rings and continue your pattern. I think you can see how this is built upon from the following diagrams.

Figures 19-15 through 19-18 show how to connect the edge rings. You can see how many rings to add from the diagrams. In Figure 19-

Figure 19-11.

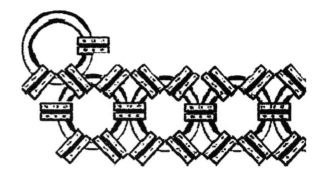

Figure 19-15.

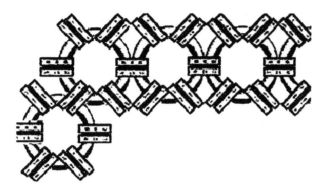

Figure 19-12.

Figure 19-16.

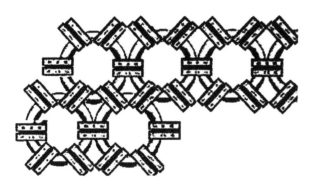

Figure 19-13.

Figure 19-17.

Figure 19-14.

Figure 19-18.

15 you add four extra small rings to the large ring you are adding; in Figure 19-16 you use two extra small rings to the large ring.

BAR MAIL

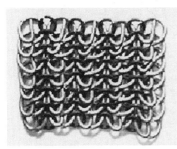

Figure 19-19.

Of course, when I heard of bar mail I had to try to make some. I took the end of a winding rod and cut a notch in it that would accommodate the wire. Placing the wire through this notch, I bent it all the way around the rod to form one link. Then I slipped it off the rod and cut it.

After that, it was simply a matter of connecting this type of link with a small link in the same manner as the 4-on-1 mail. I must admit that I do not really care much for this pattern and have not done a great deal with it.

WAVE PATTERN

I don't really consider this a new type of mail; it is just a variation in the connecting of mail. This is used in the 4-on-1 mail.

If you look closely at Figure 19-20a you will see that the mail on each side of the "wave" is reversed. In other words, the columns reverse direction. (Refer to Figure 4-1 in Chapter 4.)

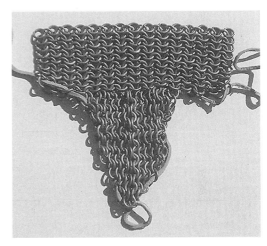

Figure 19-20b.

At the point where the two columns meet, place a ring through the top of the four rings, causing a ridge. It can be repeated as often as you like in the following columns, but it does tend to make rather lumpy mail.

Figure 19-20b shows a detail from a half-gauntlet. In this case the ridge down the back of the hand did look nice.

Figure 19-20a.

CHINESE CHAIN 1

The next two types of mail are unusual in that hey make a square chain. I have not found a method of linking them together sideways to make a square of mail, so they are used only as a long chain (Figure 19-21). They can be used for straps, handles on pouches, or watch fobs, among other things.

These are made with links all the same size. Start by taking one open link and adding four closed links to one open link. Close the link. Next take another open link and place it next to the last open link (through the same four closed links). You will have what appears in Figure 19-22.

Now you have to fold back the last two links of the chain (Figure 19-23).

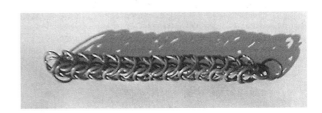

Figure 19-21.

Figure 19-22.

Figure 19-23.

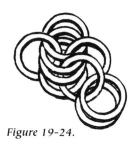

Figure 19-24.

Take one open link and add two closed links on it. Then separate the two links of the second set of links, reach through and catch the two links of the third set of links. Refer to Figure 19-24.

Next add a second link exactly like the first through the same four links. Figure 19-25 shows this link added and both of the open links folded back, one on each side. The two new closed links that were added are at the bottom of the drawing and are tucked underneath simply because I did not have anyplace else to put them.

If you take the ends of the chain and pull, you will see on the end you are working that you have two links on the end (the new closed links) at right angles to the next two links (the new open links). (Figure 19-26).

Look closely at Figure 19-26. Take ring 3 and fold it up and back. Take ring 4 and fold it down and back. Push ring 2 to the left and ring 1 to the right. As they separate rings 3 and 4 become visible between them.

Take an open link with two closed links on it. Thread the link through links 3 and 4 between links 1 and 2.

Add another open link in exactly the same place you put the last one (through all four links).

Figure 19-25.

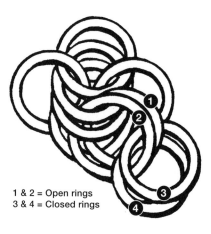

1 & 2 = Open rings
3 & 4 = Closed rings

Figure 19-26.

If you turn the chain a quarter turn you will be right back to Figure 19-26. Repeat the above steps until you have the chain the length you wish.

CHINESE CHAIN 2

This second form of chain is much like the first except that it alternates directions. Look closely at Figure 19-27. Notice the small inset in the lower left. This inset shows the alternating sets of links connected by two double links.

You start out by making the chain the same as in Chinese chain 1. So repeat the steps from Figure 19-22 to Figure 19-26.

At Figure 19-26 the difference in the two chains begins to appear. Add two more links to the end of the chain. Now you have two links (1 and 2) with two more links through them (3 and 4) and two more links through them (5 and 6). (Figure 19-28.)

Fold back links 5 and 6 on each side of the chain (Figure 19-29).

Figure 19-30: Lift up ring 3. As you do this, rings 5 and 6 slide in toward each other. Do not let them flip back again.

Figure 19-27.

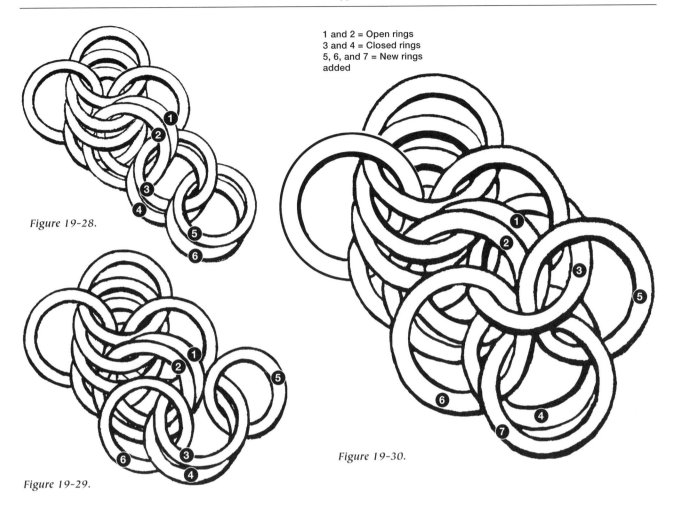

1 and 2 = Open rings
3 and 4 = Closed rings
5, 6, and 7 = New rings
added

Figure 19-28.

Figure 19-29.

Figure 19-30.

Keep them spread out to the side. Take an open ring (7) and go through rings 5 and 6 at the point where they meet in between rings 3 and 4. At this point, they are not on top of each other but only touching at the edges. If you pull on the ring you just added, you will see how the rings "fold" back on one another to form your design.

Place a second ring exactly next to this last ring, through the same rings the last ring went through. Now you have double end rings.

Next add two closed links on one open ring and go through the two end rings. At the end of your chain you now have 2-1-2. You want 2-2-2, so add another ring exactly next to the last open ring you added. Now you have 2-2-2.

Turn your chain a quarter turn. This will give you an end of the chain that is the same as in Figure 19-28. You are right back at the beginning. Just repeat the same steps.

SPIRALS

I am not altogether sure this is a form of mail, but I include instructions for it here in case you find a use for it.

This is a form of single chain. Perhaps it could be used for handles or loops on belts to hang things from. It is difficult to use it in jewelry because it is unable to move at both ends or becomes unwound and loses its look. It is possible to make necklaces with it if you can keep the coil from turning.

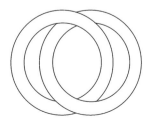

Figure 19-31.

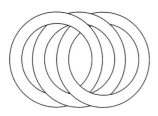

Figure 19-32.

In this pattern you use all the same size of rings to form a spiral. You add one ring at a time. Start with one closed ring on one open ring (Figure 19-31.)

Slide the rings together on top of each other. Take an open ring and go through both of the rings and close (Figure 19-32).

Lay this chain down so that the last ring you add is tilted up toward you and the first ring is tilted up away from you. Take an open ring and go up through the last ring in the chain and the middle ring (Figure 19-33).

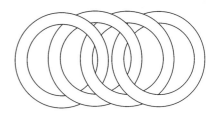

Figure 19-33.

You can start to see the spiral forming now. If you carefully pick up the chain and look at the edge, you will notice that the links all lie in the same direction. Toward the front of the chain, the link is angled away from you; toward the end of the chain, the link will be angled toward you. If this is not the case, you have one of the end links turned the wrong way. Try flipping one or the other of the end links over. It is very difficult to see clearly at this stage, but adding a few more links will make it clearer.

This last step will be repeated until you have the length of chain you desire (Figure 19-34).

Once you have several inches of chain, try turning it by holding both ends and twisting. As you can see, twisting it in one direction forms a perfect spiral (Figure 19-35). However, the other direction ends up in a mess (Figure 19-36).

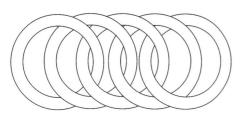

Figure 19-34.

Figure 19-37 shows the beginning of a decorative bishop's mantle made of two crosses from 6-on-2 mail joined together with a spiral at the top. The spiral will continue all around the neck area.

Figure 19-35.

Figure 19-36.

Figure 19-37.

CHAPTER 20

Photo Gallery

To finish, I have gathered some photographs of different types of mail. Figures 20-1 through 20-8 are of authentic mail from Mike Riley in Switzerland. They were taken at the Landes Museum in Zurich. The Landes Museum was once a fortress but now houses great treasures that exemplify the history of the city and canton of Zurich.

Figure 20-1. The Landes Museum.

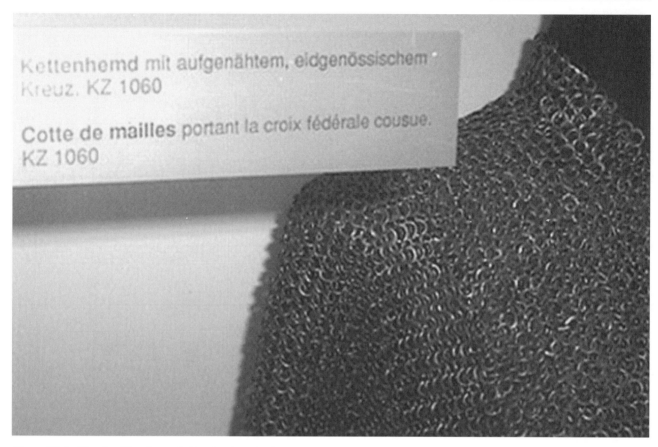

Figure 20-2. The shoulder of a mail shirt dated A.D.*1060.*

Figure 20-3. Close-up of mail from A.D. *1060. Notice the flattened wire and the rivets.*

Figure 20-4. Mail shirt from the 14th century.

Figure 20-6. A mail shirt from the 15th century.

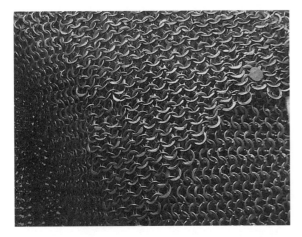

Figure 20-5. A close-up of the shoulder area of mail from the 14th century.

Figure 20-7. David getting serious in mail vest.

Figure 20-8. David modeling coif and vest.

Figure 20-9. Raven in vest.

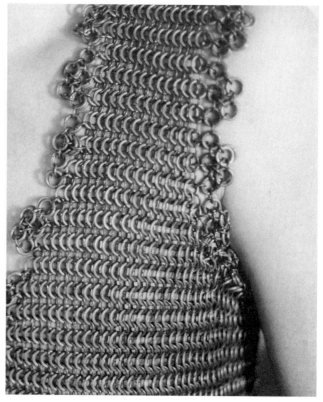

Figure 20-10. Close-up of vest.

Figure 20-11. Bill in coif.

Figure 20-12.

Figure 20-13.

Figure 20-14. "Nikki, is that you?"

Figure 20-15. Jake in large ring coif.

Figure 20-16. Bill modeling heavy coif.

Figure 20-17. David in light coif.

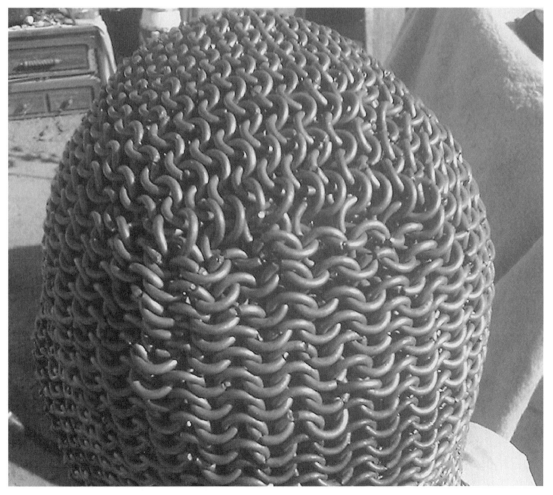

Figure 20-18.
Close-up of
square-constructed
coif.

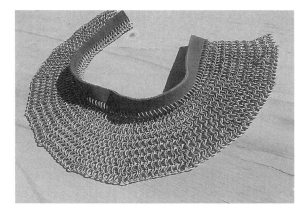

Figure 20-19. This is a camail to go on a helmet.

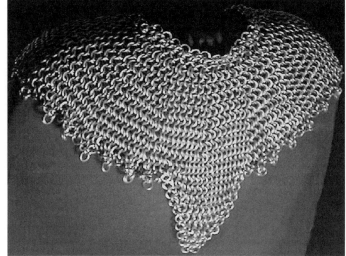

Figure 20-20.

Figure 20-21.

Figure 20-22.

Figure 20-23.

Figure 20-24.

Figure 20-25.

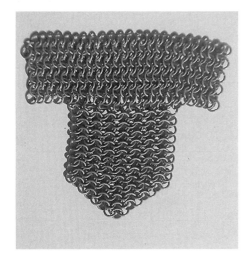

Figure 20-26.

Figure 20-27.

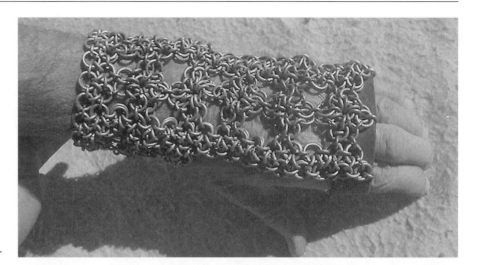

Figure 20-28.

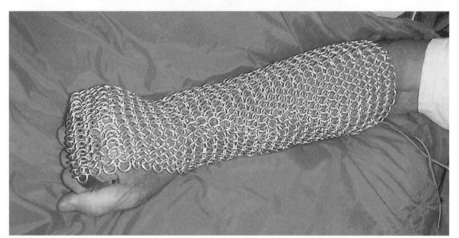

Figure 20-29.

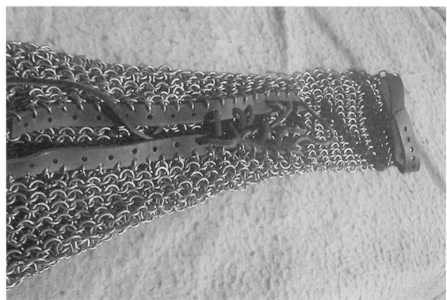

Figure 20-30.

Figure 20-31.

Figure 20-32. A pair of sabatons.

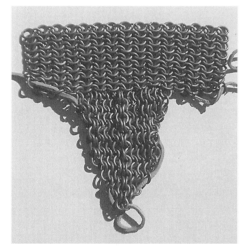

Figure 20-33.

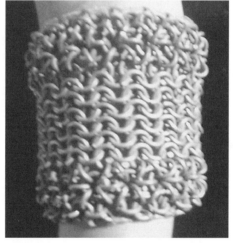

Figure 20-34. Armbands are usually worn around the upper arm near the shoulder.

Figure 20-35. Plain armband mounted on leather.

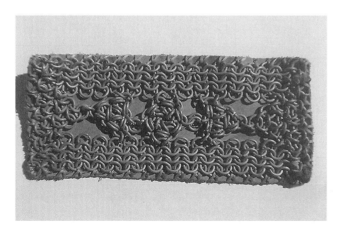

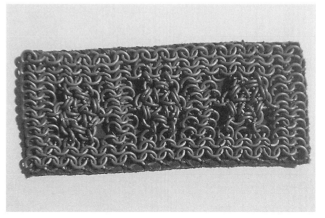

Figure 20-36. These armband designs also make a man's heavy bracelet. They could also be incorporated into a shirt pattern by repeating the square and connecting them together.

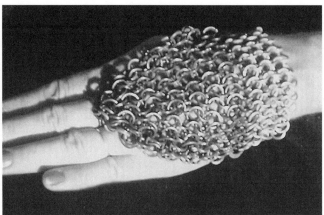

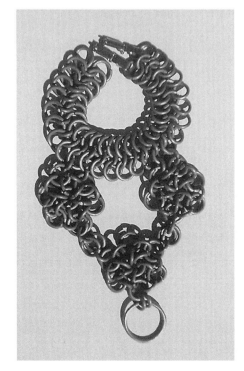

Figure 20-3.
Various handflowers.

Nikki in short headpiece.

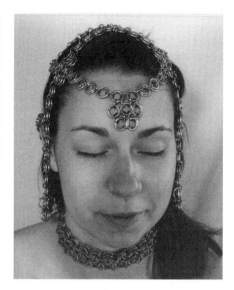

Headpiece and matching necklace worn by Christine.

Triangular headpiece.

Flower headpiece.

Figure 20-38. Various headpieces.

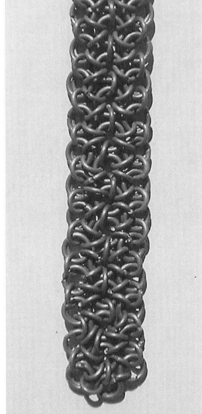

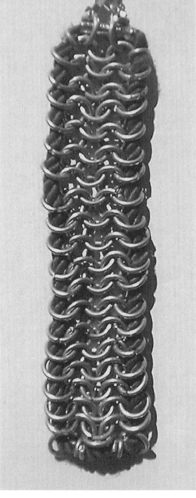

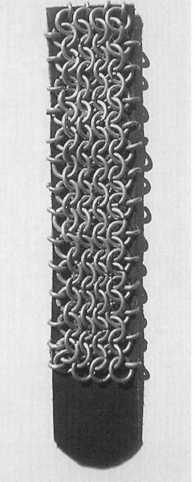

Figure 20-39. Various bracelets.

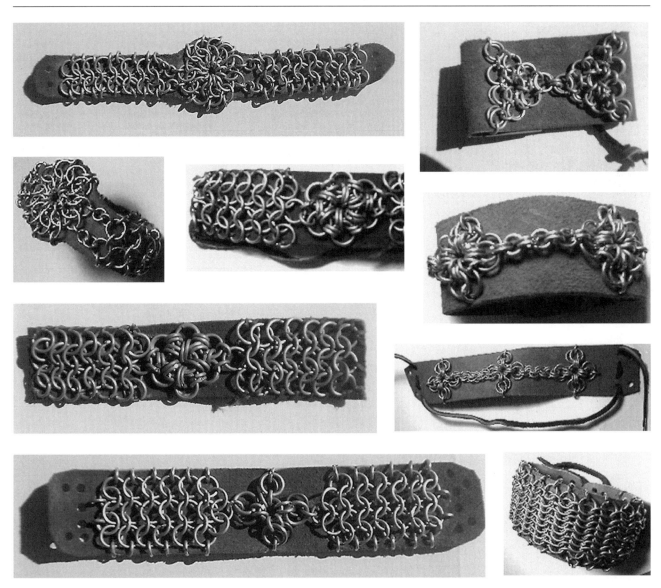

Figure 20-40. *A variety of bracelets made of mail and attached to leather. Although the designs are similar, a small change can produce a totally different look.*

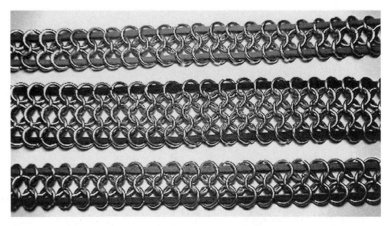

Close-up of three belts made of 4-on-1 mail with leather laced through outside rings.

Two views of a belt made with a variation of the 6-on-2 flower mounted on leather.

A matching bracelet made in the same style.

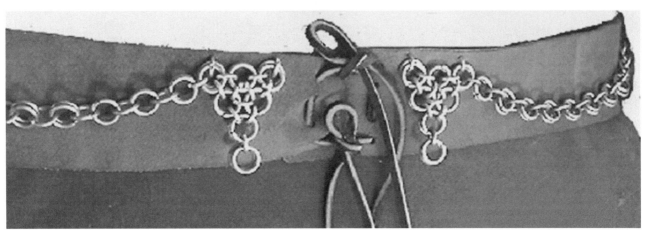

A simple but elegant 6-on-2 belt on leather.

Figure 20-41. A selection of belts.

Figure 20-42. A simple cross can be made from a variation of the 6-on-2 flower. I use this design mounted on leather to make key chains and necklaces on leather thongs.

Figure 20-43. Several variations of small bags made of 4-on-1 mail in front and leather on back.

Figure 20-44. Various necklace designs.

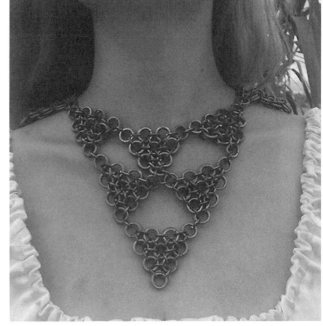

Figure 20-45. Various shoulder necklace designs.

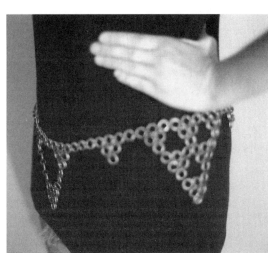